THE ESSENTIAL

EMMA GOLDMAN

First Warbler Press Edition 2022

Foreword © 2022 Vivian Gornick

Biographical Timeline © Warbler Press

First published: "What I Believe," *New York World,* July 19, 1908 | "Anarchism: What It Really Stands For," *Anarchism and Other Essays*, New York: Mother Earth Publishing Co., 1910 | "The Psychology of Political Violence," *Anarchism and Other Essays*, New York: Mother Earth Publishing Co., 1910 | "The Individual, Society and the State," from pamphlet, *The Place of the Individual in Society*, Chicago: Free Society Forum, 1940 | "The Traffic in Women," *Anarchism and Other Essays*, New York: Mother Earth Publishing Co., 1910 | "Marriage and Love," *Anarchism and Other Essays*, New York: Mother Earth Publishing Co., 1910 | "The Tragedy of Woman's Emancipation," *Anarchism and Other Essays*, New York: Mother Earth Publishing Co., 1910 | "Victims of Morality," *Mother Earth,* March 1913 | "Prisons: A Social Crime and Failure," *Anarchism and Other Essays*, New York: Mother Earth Publishing Co., 1910 | "Minorities Versus Majorities," *Anarchism and Other Essays*, New York: Mother Earth Publishing Co., 1910 | "Patriotism: A Menace to Liberty," *Anarchism and Other Essays*, New York: Mother Earth Publishing Co., 1910 | "Intellectual Proletarians," *Mother Earth,* February 1914 | Nelly Bly interview of Emma Goldman, *New York World,* September 17, 1893

ISBN 978-1-959891-07-9 (paperback)
ISBN 978-1-959891-08-6 (e-book)

Library of Congress Control Number: 2022942050

warblerpress.com

THE ESSENTIAL

EMMA GOLDMAN

Anarchism
Feminism
Liberation

EMMA GOLDMAN

Foreword by VIVIAN GORNICK

Selected and Edited by ULRICH BAER and NATASHA ROY

warbler press

CONTENTS

FOREWORD
by Vivian Gornick

EMMA GOLDMAN WAS not a thinker, she was an incarnation. Hers was the sensibility not of the intellectual but of the artist; and she performed like an artist, dramatizing for others what they could hardly articulate for themselves. To hear Emma describe, in language as magnetic as it was illuminating, what the boot felt like on the neck was to feel the mythic quality of organized oppression. It made you *see* yourself in history. That insight eased the heart and clarified the spirit. To clarify was to gain courage; and courage, if nothing else, was an exhilaration. Through Emma's performance, anarchism did what Russian novelist Leo Tolstoy said a work of art should do: it made people love life more.

Goldman was regularly being taken to task by her fellow anarchists for interpreting anarchism as a movement for individual self-expression rather than as a collective bent on overthrowing corporate capitalism. To this critique she would reply hotly that if radicals gave up sex and art while making the new world they would become devoid of joy. Without joy, human beings would cease being human—and then any world they made would be even more heartless than it had been before. In conclusion, as she herself said, if she couldn't dance, Emma wasn't coming to their revolution.

A handful of radicals throughout the centuries have intuited that a successful revolution includes a healthy passion for the inner life. In service to this insight Emma Goldman became eloquent in defense of causes—sexual freedom, marriage reform, organized labor—that a majority of her fellow anarchists declared trivial. For Emma, however, they were emblematic of deprivations she thought no human being could or should have to live with. It was precisely on behalf of free love, marital equality, and decent working conditions that she was proud to call herself an anarchist. To retreat from *this* agenda, she insisted, was to ensure political disaster.

It was the intensity with which she declared herself—in lecture halls, on open-air platforms, in school auditoriums and private homes, from theatre stages and prison cells, the back of a truck or a courtroom stand—that made her world famous. That intensity was midwife to a remarkable gift she had for making those who heard her feel intimately connected to the pain inherent in whatever social condition she was denouncing. As the women and men in her audience listened to her, a scenario of almost mythic proportions seemed to unfold before their eyes. The homeliness of their own small lives became invested with a sense of drama that acted as a catalyst for the wild, vagrant hope that things need not be as they were.

This ability to make vivid the distress of living under the arbitrary rule of institutional power—Goldman's eternal subject, no matter the title of the lecture—originated in an ingrained sense of oppression that burned as brightly in her at the end of her life as it did at the beginning. The story of that life as she told it, set against a background of Russian despotism, Jewish marginality, and filial lovelessness, was one long tale of protest, not so much against poverty and discrimination (although there was plenty of that), as against a perception, there from earliest times, that some inborn right to begin and end with herself was forever being thwarted. There seemed always to be those in a position of authority to exercise restraint *unfairly, and for no real reason* over those who were not free to throw it off. She had always felt the situation puzzling and unjust; and in her, such was her disposition, that injustice burned unbearably. It was the "unbearably" that set her apart.

For Emma, *felt* was the operative word. She always claimed that the ideas of anarchism were of secondary use if grasped only with one's reasoning intelligence; it was necessary to "feel them in every fiber like a flame, a consuming fever, an elemental passion." This, in essence, was the core of Goldman's radicalism: an impassioned faith, lodged in the nervous system, that feelings were everything. Radical politics for her was, in fact, the history of one's own hurt, thwarted, humiliated feelings at the hands of institutionalized authority. Handed down from on high, such authority was to be fought at all times, in all places, with all one's might. It was from this single-minded article of faith—one that neither gained nuance nor lost force—that Emma never departed; and it is upon its basic appeal to every movement for social justice that ever was that she is able to command the attention of the contemporary reader.

⌣

Anarchism is the political philosophy that comes closest to addressing the anguish of the stifled spirit, and in Emma Goldman it found it visceral embodiment. Social injustice may or may not have been the cause of, or the explanation for, her exorbitant sense of insult in the face of power ill-used, but it surely was its intimate. It was not even the injustice itself that she found so oppressive, it was being forced to *submit* to it without recourse to opposition; that was the human right that was at stake. To accept the denial of that right was to surrender something vital to one's humanity: that which supplied the difference between those who walked the earth upright and those who crawled on all fours. It was with those who shared this value that, all her years, she felt most alive. The world of the utopian anarchist future held much less

FOREWORD ix

reality for her than the one in which she fought daily to secure the rights of the rebel and the dissenter.

For this reason alone she loved the United States more than any other country she lived in. She loved passionately the essence of homegrown U.S. radicalism; never stopped being amazed at and delighted by the American appetite for protest as, time and again, she saw one part of the body politic or another rise up to claim what the democracy had promised but failed to deliver. With all its capitalist brutality, America was where the rebel seemed most unconquerable.

In Emma Goldman we have a prototype of the European anarchist crucially influenced by the American insistence on individuation. Had she been alive in the 1960s she would have been as inspired by the rise of the new left and the liberationist movements—especially Gay Rights and Women's Rights—as they were by her. And even now, forty years down the road, when these movements are still struggling to achieve lasting change, she would be gratified to see thousands of young Americans militantly engaged by them, as well as by the more current issues of planetary threat, transgender discrimination, rising economic inequality and, of course, the never-ending blight of homegrown racism. How happily Emma would have climbed the barricades on behalf of any or all of these social miseries!

Probably the most influential chant of the 1960s and '70s was "the personal is political." To this day this is the phrase that has conjured the noble enterprise of struggling against permanent odds to achieve a world in which a healthy respect for life on the ground occupies center stage. It is also the phrase that most deserves to be associated—in fear, hope, and excitement—with the legacy of Emma Goldman.

WHAT I BELIEVE
by Emma Goldman

"What I believe" has many times been the target of hack writers. Such blood-curdling and incoherent stories have been circulated about me, it is no wonder that the average human being has palpitation of the heart at the very mention of the name Emma Goldman. It is too bad that we no longer live in the times when witches were burned at the stake or tortured to drive the evil spirit out of them. For, indeed, Emma Goldman is a witch! True, she does not eat little children, but she does many worse things. She manufactures bombs and gambles in crowned heads. B-r-r-r!

Such is the impression the public has of myself and my beliefs. It is therefore very much to the credit of *The World* that it gives its readers at least an opportunity to learn what my beliefs really are.

The student of the history of progressive thought is well aware that every idea in its early stages has been misrepresented, and the adherents of such ideas have been maligned and persecuted. One need not go back two thousand years to the time when those who believed in the gospel of Jesus were thrown into the arena or hunted into dungeons to realize how little great beliefs or earnest believers are understood. The history of progress is written in the blood of men and women who have dared to espouse an unpopular cause, as, for instance, the black man's right to his body, or woman's right to her soul. If, then, from time immemorial, the New has met with opposition and condemnation, why should my beliefs be exempt from a crown of thorns?

"What I believe" is a process rather than a finality. Finalities are for gods and governments, not for the human intellect. While it may be true that Herbert Spencer's formulation of liberty is the most important on the subject, as a political basis of society, yet life is something more than formulas. In the battle for freedom, as Ibsen has so well pointed out, it is the *struggle* for, not so much the attainment of, liberty, that develops all that is strongest, sturdiest and finest in human character.

Anarchism is not only a process, however, that marches on with "sombre steps," coloring all that is positive and constructive in organic development. It is a conspicuous protest of the most militant type. It is so absolutely uncompromising, insisting and permeating a force as to overcome the most stubborn assault and to withstand the criticism of those who really constitute the last trumpets of a decaying age.

Anarchists are by no means passive spectators in the theatre of social development; on the contrary, they have some very positive notions as regards aims and methods.

That I may make myself as clear as possible without using too much space, permit me to adopt the topical mode of treatment of "What I Believe":

I. AS TO PROPERTY

"Property" means dominion over things and the denial to others of the use of those things. So long as production was not equal to the normal demand, institutional property may have had some *raison d'être*. One has only to consult economics, however, to know that the productivity of labor within the last few decades has increased so tremendously as to exceed normal demand a hundred-fold, and to make property not only a hindrance to human well-being, but an obstacle, a deadly barrier, to all progress. It is the private dominion over things that condemns millions of people to be mere nonentities, living corpses without originality or power of initiative, human machines of flesh and blood, who pile up mountains of wealth for others and pay for it with a gray, dull and wretched existence for themselves. I believe that there can be no real wealth, social wealth, so long as it rests on human lives—young lives, old lives and lives in the making.

It is conceded by all radical thinkers that the fundamental cause of this terrible state of affairs is (1) that man must sell his labor; (2) that his inclination and judgment are subordinated to the will of a master.

Anarchism is the only philosophy that can and will do away with this humiliating and degrading situation. It differs from all other theories inasmuch as it points out that man's development, his physical well-being, his latent qualities and innate disposition alone must determine the character and conditions of his work. Similarly will one's physical and mental appreciations and his soul cravings decide how much he shall consume. To make this a reality will, I believe, be possible only in a society based on voluntary co-operation of productive groups, communities and societies loosely federated together, eventually developing into a free communism, actuated by a solidarity of interests. There can be no freedom in the large sense of the word, no harmonious development, so long as mercenary and commercial considerations play an important part in the determination of personal conduct.

II. AS TO GOVERNMENT

I believe government, organized authority, or the State is necessary *only* to maintain or protect property and monopoly. It has proven efficient in that function only. As a promoter of individual liberty, human well-being and social harmony, which alone constitute real order, government stands condemned by all the great men of the world.

I therefore believe, with my fellow-Anarchists, that the statutory regulations, legislative enactments, constitutional provisions, are invasive. They never yet induced man to do anything he could and would not do by virtue of his intellect or temperament, nor prevented anything that man was impelled to do by the same dictates. Millet's pictorial description of "The Man with the Hoe," Meunier's masterpieces of the miners that have aided in lifting labor from its degrading position, Gorki's descriptions of the underworld, Ibsen's psychological analysis of human life, could never have been induced by government any more than the spirit which impels a man to save a drowning child or a crippled woman from a burning building has ever been called into operation by statutory regulations or the policeman's club. I believe—indeed, I know—that whatever is fine and beautiful in the human expresses and asserts itself in spite of government, and not because of it.

The Anarchists are therefore justified in assuming that Anarchism—the absence of government—will insure the widest and greatest scope for unhampered human development, the cornerstone of true social progress and harmony.

As to the stereotyped argument that government acts as a check on crime and vice, even the makers of law no longer believe it. This country spends millions of dollars for the maintenance of her "criminals" behind prison bars, yet crime is on the increase. Surely this state of affairs is not owing to an insufficiency of laws! Ninety percent of all crimes are property crimes, which have their root in our economic iniquities. So long as these latter continue to exist we might convert every lamp-post into a gibbet without having the least effect on the crime in our midst. Crimes resulting from heredity can certainly never be cured by law. Surely we are learning even today that such crimes can effectively be treated only by the best modern medical methods at our command, and, above all, by the spirit of a deeper sense of fellowship, kindness and understanding.

III. AS TO MILITARISM

I should not treat of this subject separately, since it belongs to the paraphernalia of government, if it were not for the fact that those who are most vigorously opposed to my beliefs on the ground that the latter stand for force are the advocates of militarism.

The fact is that Anarchists are the only true advocates of peace, the only people who call a halt to the growing tendency of militarism, which is fast making of this erstwhile free country an imperialistic and despotic power.

The military spirit is the most merciless, heartless and brutal in existence. It fosters an institution for which there is not even a pretense of justification. The soldier, to quote Tolstoi, is a professional man-killer. He does not kill for the love of it, like a savage, or in a passion, like a homicide. He is a cold-blooded, mechanical, obedient tool of his military superiors. He is ready to cut throats or scuttle a ship at the command of his ranking officer, without knowing or, perhaps, caring how, why or wherefore. I am supported in this contention by no less a military light than Gen. Funston. I quote from the latter's communication to the *New York Evening Post* of June 30, dealing with the case of Private William Buwalda, which caused such a stir all through the Northwest.[1] "The first duty of an officer or enlisted man," says our noble warrior, "is unquestioning obedience and loyalty to the government to which he has sworn allegiance; it makes no difference whether he approves of that government or not."

How can we harmonize the principle of "unquestioning obedience" with the principle of "life, liberty and the pursuit of happiness"? The deadly power of militarism has never before been so effectually demonstrated in this country as in the recent condemnation by court-martial of William Buwalda, of San Francisco, Company A, Engineers, to five years in military prison. Here was a man who had a record of fifteen years of continuous service. "His character and conduct were unimpeachable," we are told by Gen. Funston, who, in consideration of it, reduced Buwalda's sentence to three years. Yet the man is thrown suddenly out of the army, dishonored, robbed of his chances of a pension and sent to prison. What was his crime? Just listen, ye free-born Americans! William Buwalda attended a public meeting, and after the lecture he shook hands with the speaker. Gen. Funston, in his letter to the *Post*, to which I have already referred above, asserts that Buwalda's action was a "great military offense, infinitely worse than desertion." In another public statement, which the General made in Portland, Ore., he said that "Buwalda's was a serious crime, equal to treason."

It is quite true that the meeting had been arranged by Anarchists. Had the Socialists issued the call, Gen. Funston informs us, there would have been no objection to Buwalda's presence. Indeed, the General says, "I would not have the slightest hesitancy about attending a Socialist meeting myself." But to attend an Anarchist meeting with Emma Goldman as speaker—could there be anything more "treasonable"?

For this horrible crime a man, a free-born American citizen, who has given this country the best fifteen years of his life, and whose character and conduct during that time were "unimpeachable," is now languishing in a prison, dishonored, disgraced and robbed of a livelihood.

Can there be anything more destructive of the true genius of liberty than the spirit that made Buwalda's sentence possible—the spirit of unquestioning obedience? Is it for this that the American people have in the last few years sacrificed four hundred

---

1   [All notes added by the editors of this edition.] William Buwalda (1869–1946) was a United States soldier who gained national attention after being court-martialed and sentenced to three years' hard labor for shaking hands with Emma Goldman after one of her public speeches given on April 26, 1908. He claimed to have attended the lecture out of curiosity and was sentenced for disloyalty to the government. Goldman and others made public efforts to free Buwalda, who was pardoned by President Theodore Roosevelt ten months after the sentence had been passed.

million dollars and their hearts' blood?

I believe that militarism—a standing army and navy in any country—is indicative of the decay of liberty and of the destruction of all that is best and finest in our nation. The steadily growing clamor for more battleships and an increased army on the ground that these guarantee us peace is as absurd as the argument that the peaceful man is he who goes well armed.

The same lack of consistency is displayed by those peace pretenders who oppose Anarchism because it supposedly teaches violence, and who would yet be delighted over the possibility of the American nation soon being able to hurl dynamite bombs upon defenseless enemies from flying machines.

I believe that militarism will cease when the liberty-loving spirits of the world say to their masters: "Go and do your own killing. We have sacrificed ourselves and our loved ones long enough fighting your battles. In return you have made parasites and criminals of us in times of peace and brutalized us in times of war. You have separated us from our brothers and have made of the world a human slaughterhouse. No, we will not do your killing or fight for the country that you have stolen from us."

Oh, I believe with all my heart that human brotherhood and solidarity will clear the horizon from the terrible red streak of war and destruction.

IV. AS TO FREE SPEECH AND PRESS

The Buwalda case is only one phase of the larger question of free speech, free press and the right of free assembly.

Many good people imagine that the principles of free speech or press can be exercised properly and with safety within the limits of constitutional guarantees. That is the only excuse, it seems to me, for the terrible apathy and indifference to the onslaught upon free speech and press that we have witnessed in this country within the last few months.

I believe that free speech and press mean that I may say and write what I please. This right, when regulated by constitutional provisions, legislative enactments, almighty decisions of the Postmaster General or the policeman's club, becomes a farce. I am well aware that I will be warned of consequences if we remove the chains from speech and press. I believe, however, that the cure of consequences resulting from the unlimited exercise of expression is to allow more expression.

Mental shackles have never yet stemmed the tide of progress, whereas premature social explosions have only too often been brought about through a wave of repression.

Will our governors never learn that countries like England, Holland, Norway, Sweden and Denmark, with the largest freedom of expression, have been freest from "consequences"? Whereas Russia, Spain, Italy, France and, alas! even America, have raised these "consequences" to the most pressing political factor. Ours is supposed to be a country ruled by the majority, yet every policeman who is not vested with power by the majority can break up a meeting, drag the lecturer off the platform and club the audience out of the hall in true Russian fashion. The Postmaster General, who is not an elective officer, has the power to suppress publications and confiscate mail. From his decision there is no more appeal than from that of the Russian Czar. Truly, I believe we need a new Declaration of Independence. Is there no modern Jefferson or Adams?

V. AS TO THE CHURCH

At the recent convention of the political remnants of a once revolutionary idea it was voted that religion and vote getting have nothing to do with each other. Why should they? So long as man is willing to delegate to the devil the care of his soul, he might, with the same consistency, delegate to the politician the care of his rights. That religion is a private affair has long been settled by the Bis-Marxian Socialists of Germany. Our American Marxians, poor of blood and originality, must needs go to Germany for their wisdom. That wisdom has served as a capital whip to lash the several millions of people into the well-disciplined army of Socialism. It might do the same here. For goodness' sake, let's not offend respectability, let's not hurt the religious feelings of the people.

Religion is a superstition that originated in man's mental inability to solve natural phenomena. The Church is an organized institution that has always been a stumbling block to progress.

Organized churchism has stripped religion of its naïveté and primitiveness. It has turned religion into a nightmare that oppresses the human soul and holds the mind in bondage. "The Dominion of Darkness," as the last true Christian, Leo Tolstoi, calls the Church, has been a foe of human development and free thought, and as such it has no place in the life of a truly free people.

VI. AS TO MARRIAGE AND LOVE

I believe these are probably the most tabooed subjects in this country. It is almost impossible to talk about them without scandalizing the cherished propriety of a lot of good folk. No wonder so much ignorance prevails relative to these questions. Nothing short of an open, frank, and intelligent discussion will purify the air from the hysterical, sentimental rubbish that is shrouding these vital subjects, vital to individual as well as social well-being.

Marriage and love are not synonymous; on the contrary, they are often antagonistic to each other. I am aware of the fact that some marriages are actuated by love, but the narrow, material confines of marriage, as it is, speedily crush the tender flower of affection.

Marriage is an institution which furnishes the State and Church with a tremendous revenue and the means of prying into that phase of life which refined people have long considered their own, their very own most sacred affair. Love is that most powerful factor of human relationship which from time immemorial has defied all man-made laws and broken through the iron bars of conventions in Church and morality. Marriage is often an economic arrangement purely, furnishing the woman with a life-long life insurance policy and the man with a perpetuator of his kind or a pretty toy. That is, marriage, or the training thereto, prepares the woman for the life of a parasite, a dependent, helpless servant, while it furnishes the man the right of a chattel mortgage over a human life.

How can such a condition of affairs have anything in common with love?—with the element that would forego all the wealth of money and power and live in its own world of untrammeled human expression? But this is not the age of romanticism, of Romeo and Juliet, Faust and Marguerite, of moonlight ecstasies, of flowers and songs. Ours is a practical age. Our first consideration is an income. So much the worse for us if we have reached the era when the soul's highest flights are to be checked. No race can develop without the love element.

But if two people are to worship at the shrine of love, what is to become of the golden calf, marriage? "It is the only security for the woman, for the child, the family, the State." But it is no security to love; and without love no true home can or does exist. Without love no child should be born; without love no true woman can be related to a man. The fear that love is not sufficient material safety for the child is out of date. I believe when woman signs her own emancipation, her first declaration of independence will consist in admiring and loving a man for the qualities of his heart and mind and not for the quantities in his pocket. The second declaration will be that she has the right to follow that love without let or hindrance from the outside world. The third and most important declaration will be the absolute right to free motherhood.

In such a mother and an equally free father rests the safety of the child. They have the strength, the sturdiness, the harmony to create an atmosphere wherein alone the human plant can grow into an exquisite flower.

VII. AS TO ACTS OF VIOLENCE

And now I have come to that point in my beliefs about which the greatest misunderstanding prevails in the minds of the American public. "Well, come, now, don't you propagate violence, the killing of crowned heads and Presidents?" Who says that I do? Have you heard me, has anyone heard me? Has anyone seen it printed in our literature? No, but the papers say so, everybody says so; consequently it must be so. Oh, for the accuracy and logic of the dear public!

I believe that Anarchism is the only philosophy of peace, the only theory of the social relationship that values human life above everything else. I know that some Anarchists have committed acts of violence, but it is the terrible economic inequality and great political injustice that prompt such acts, not Anarchism. Every institution today rests on violence; our very atmosphere is saturated with it. So long as such a state exists we might as well strive to stop the rush of Niagara as hope to do away with violence. I have already stated that countries with some measure of freedom of expression have had few or no acts of violence. What is the moral? Simply this: No act committed by an Anarchist has been for personal gain, aggrandizement or profit, but rather a conscious protest against some repressive, arbitrary, tyrannical measure from above.

President Carnot, of France, was killed by Caserio in response to Carnot's refusal to commute the death sentence of Vaillant, for whose life the entire literary, scientific and humanitarian world of France had pleaded.[2]

Bresci went to Italy on his own money, earned in the silk weaving mills of Paterson, to call King Humbert to the bar of justice for his order to shoot defenseless women and children during a bread riot.[3] Angelino executed Prime Minister Canovas for the latter's resurrection of the Spanish inquisition at Montjuich Prison. Alexander Berkman attempted the life of Henry C. Frick during the Homestead strike[4] only because of his intense sympathy for the eleven strikers killed by Pinkertons and for the widows and orphans evicted by Frick from their wretched little homes that were owned by Mr. Carnegie.

Every one of these men not only made his reasons known to the world in spoken or written statements, showing the cause that led to his act, proving that the unbearable economic and political pressure, the suffering and despair of their fellow-men, women and children prompted the acts, and not the philosophy of Anarchism. They came openly, frankly and ready to stand the consequences, ready to give their own lives.

In diagnosing the true nature of our social disease I cannot condemn those who, through no fault of their own, are suffering from a wide-spread malady.

---

2   Sante Geronimo Caserio (1873–1894), Italian anarchist who assassinated the President of the French Republic, Marie François Sadi Carnot, in 1894.

3   Gaetano Bresci (1869–1901), Italian-American anarchist who in 1900 assassinated King Umberto I of Italy, under whose reign dozens of workers had been murdered during bread riots in Milan in 1898. Michele Angiolillo Lombardi (1871–1897), an Italian anarchist who assassinated Spanish Prime Minister Antonio Cánovas del Castillo in 1897; he was executed by Spanish authorities that year. Alexander (Sasha) Berkman (1870–1936), Russian-American anarchist, author, and one-time lover and lifelong friend of Goldman's. In 1892, Berkman made an unsuccessful attempt to assassinate industrialist Henry Clay Frick, for which he served fourteen years in prison.

4   The 1892 Homestead Strike was a violent dispute between the Carnegie Steel Company and the Amalgamated Association of Iron and Steel Workers Union in Homestead, Pennsylvania. It was a response to the Company's discharge of union workers and was one of the deadliest labor-management conflicts in the nation's history. The violent strike led to the government interceding on behalf of a corporation against a union.

I do not believe that these acts can, or ever have been intended to, bring about the social reconstruction. That can only be done, first, by a broad and wide education as to man's place in society and his proper relation to his fellows; and, second, through example. By example I mean the actual living of a truth once recognized, not the mere theorizing of its life element. Lastly, and the most powerful weapon, is the conscious, intelligent, organized, economic protest of the masses through direct action and the general strike.

The general contention that Anarchists are opposed to organization, and hence stand for chaos, is absolutely groundless. True, we do not believe in the compulsory, arbitrary side of organization that would compel people of antagonistic tastes and interests into a body and hold them there by coercion. Organization as the result of natural blending of common interests, brought about through voluntary adhesion, Anarchists do not only not oppose, but believe in as the only possible basis of social life.

It is the harmony of organic growth which produces variety of color and form—the complete whole we admire in the flower. Analogously will the organized activity of free human beings endowed with the spirit of solidarity result in the perfection of social harmony—which is Anarchism. Indeed, only Anarchism makes non-authoritarian organization a reality, since it abolishes the existing antagonism between individuals and classes.

ANARCHISM

ANARCHISM: WHAT IT REALLY STANDS FOR

ANARCHY.

Ever reviled, accursed, ne'er understood,
Thou art the grisly terror of our age.
"Wreck of all order," cry the multitude,
"Art thou, and war and murder's endless rage."
O, let them cry. To them that ne'er have striven
The truth that lies behind a word to find,
To them the word's right meaning was not given.
They shall continue blind among the blind.
But thou, O word, so clear, so strong, so pure,
Thou sayest all which I for goal have taken.
I give thee to the future! Thine secure
When each at least unto himself shall waken.
Comes it in sunshine? In the tempest's thrill?
I cannot tell—but it the earth shall see!
I am an Anarchist! Wherefore I will
Not rule, and also ruled I will not be!

JOHN HENRY MACKAY.

T HE HISTORY OF human growth and development is at the same time the history of the terrible struggle of every new idea heralding the approach of a brighter dawn. In its tenacious hold on tradition, the Old has never hesitated to make use of the foulest and cruelest means to stay the advent of the New, in whatever form or period the latter may have asserted itself. Nor need we retrace our steps into the distant past to realize the enormity of opposition, difficulties, and hardships placed in the path of every progressive idea. The rack, the thumbscrew, and the knout are still with us; so are the convict's garb and the social wrath, all conspiring against the spirit that is serenely marching on.

Anarchism could not hope to escape the fate of all other ideas of innovation. Indeed, as the most revolutionary and uncompromising innovator, Anarchism must needs meet with the combined ignorance and venom of the world it aims to reconstruct.

To deal even remotely with all that is being said and done against Anarchism would necessitate the writing of a whole volume. I shall therefore meet only two of the principal objections. In so doing, I shall attempt to elucidate what Anarchism really stands for.

The strange phenomenon of the opposition to Anarchism is that it brings to light the relation between so-called intelligence and ignorance. And yet this is not so very strange when we consider the relativity of all things. The ignorant mass has in its favor that it makes no pretense of knowledge or tolerance. Acting, as it always does, by mere impulse, its reasons are like those of a child. "Why?" "Because." Yet the opposition of the uneducated to Anarchism deserves the same consideration as that of the intelligent man.

What, then, are the objections? First, Anarchism is impractical, though a beautiful ideal. Second, Anarchism stands for violence and destruction, hence it must be repudiated as vile and dangerous. Both the intelligent man and the ignorant mass judge not from a thorough knowledge of the subject, but either from hearsay or false interpretation.

A practical scheme, says Oscar Wilde, is either one already in existence, or a scheme that could be carried out under the existing conditions; but it is exactly the existing conditions that one objects to, and any scheme that could accept these conditions is wrong and foolish. The true criterion of the practical, therefore, is not whether the latter can keep intact the wrong or foolish; rather is it whether the scheme has vitality enough to leave the stagnant waters of the old, and build, as well as sustain, new life. In the light of this conception, Anarchism is indeed practical. More than any other idea, it is helping to do away with the wrong and foolish; more than any other idea, it is building and sustaining new life.

The emotions of the ignorant man are continuously kept at a pitch by the most blood-curdling stories about Anarchism. Not a thing too outrageous to be employed against this philosophy and its exponents. Therefore Anarchism represents to the unthinking what the proverbial bad man does to the child,—a black monster bent on swallowing everything; in short, destruction and violence.

Destruction and violence! How is the ordinary man to know that the most violent element in society is ignorance; that its power of destruction is the very thing Anarchism is combating? Nor is he aware that Anarchism, whose roots, as it were, are part of nature's forces, destroys, not healthful tissue, but parasitic growths that feed on the life's essence of society. It is merely clearing the soil from weeds and sagebrush, that it may eventually bear healthy fruit.

Someone has said that it requires less mental effort to condemn than to think. The widespread mental indolence, so prevalent in society, proves this to be only too true. Rather than to go to the bottom of any given idea, to examine into its origin and meaning, most people will either condemn it altogether, or rely on some superficial or prejudicial definition of non-essentials.

Anarchism urges man to think, to investigate, to analyze every proposition; but that the brain capacity of the average reader be not taxed too much, I also shall begin with a definition, and then elaborate on the latter.

ANARCHISM:—The philosophy of a new social order based on liberty unrestricted by man-made law; the theory that all forms of government rest on violence, and are therefore wrong and harmful, as well as unnecessary.

The new social order rests, of course, on the materialistic basis of life; but while all Anarchists agree that the main evil today is an economic one, they maintain that the solution of that evil can be brought about only through the consideration of *every phase* of life,—individual, as well as the collective; the internal, as well as the external phases.

A thorough perusal of the history of human development will disclose two elements in bitter conflict with each other; elements that are only now beginning to be understood, not as foreign to each other, but as closely related and truly harmonious, if only placed in proper environment: the individual and social instincts. The individual and society have waged a relentless and bloody battle for ages, each striving for supremacy, because each was blind to the value and importance of the other. The individual and social instincts,—the one a most potent factor for individual endeavor, for growth, aspiration, self-realization; the other an equally potent factor for mutual helpfulness and social well-being.

The explanation of the storm raging within the individual; and between him and his surroundings, is not far to seek. The primitive man, unable to understand his being, much less the unity of all life, felt himself absolutely dependent on blind, hidden forces ever ready to mock and taunt him. Out of that attitude grew the religious concepts of man as a mere speck of dust dependent on superior powers on high, who can only be appeased by complete surrender. All the early sagas rest on that idea, which continues to be the *Leitmotiv* of the biblical tales dealing with the relation of man to God, to the State, to society. Again and again the same motif, *man is nothing, the powers are everything.* Thus Jehovah would only endure man on condition of complete surrender. Man can have all the glories of the earth, but he must not become conscious of himself. The State, society, and moral laws all sing the same refrain: Man can have all the glories of the earth, but he must not become conscious of himself.

Anarchism is the only philosophy which brings to man the consciousness of himself; which maintains that God, the State, and society are non-existent, that their promises are null and void, since they can be fulfilled only through man's subordination. Anarchism is therefore the teacher of the unity of life; not merely in nature, but in man. There is no conflict between the individual and the social instincts, any more than there is between the heart and the lungs: the one the receptacle of a precious life essence, the other the repository of the element that keeps the essence pure and strong. The individual is the heart of society, conserving the essence of social life; society is the lungs, which are distributing the element to keep the life essence—that is, the individual—pure and strong.

"The one thing of value in the world," says Emerson, "is the active soul; this every man contains within him. The soul active sees absolute truth and utters truth and creates."[5] In other worlds, the individual instinct is the thing of value in the world. It is the true soul that sees and creates the truth alive, out of which is to come a still greater truth, the re-born social soul.

Anarchism is the great liberator of man from the phantoms that have held him captive; it is the arbiter and pacifier of the two forces for individual and social harmony. To accomplish that unity, Anarchism has declared war on the pernicious influences which have so far prevented the harmonious blending of individual and social instincts, the individual and society.

Religion, the dominion of the human mind; Property, the dominion of human needs; and Government, the dominion of human conduct, represent the stronghold of man's enslavement and all the horrors it entails. Religion! How it dominates man's mind, how it humiliates and degrades his soul. God is everything, man is nothing, says religion. But out of that nothing God has created a kingdom so despotic, so tyrannical, so cruel, so terribly exacting that naught but gloom and tears and blood have ruled the world since gods began. Anarchism rouses man to rebellion against this black monster. Break your mental fetters, says Anarchism to man, for not until you think and judge for yourself will you get rid of the dominion of darkness, the greatest obstacle to all progress.

Property, the dominion of man's needs, the denial of the right to satisfy his needs. Time was when property claimed a divine right, when it came to man with the same refrain, even as religion, "Sacrifice! Abnegate! Submit!" The spirit of Anarchism has lifted man from his prostrate position. He now stands erect, with his face toward the light. He has learned to see the insatiable, devouring, devastating nature of property, and he is preparing to strike the monster dead.

"Property is robbery," said the great French Anarchist Proudhon.[6] Yes, but without risk and danger to the robber. Monopolizing the accumulated efforts of man, property has robbed him of his birthright, and has turned him loose a pauper and an outcast. Property has not even the time-worn excuse that man does not create enough to satisfy all needs. The A B C student of economics knows that the productivity of

---

5   Ralph Waldo Emerson, "The American Scholar," lecture first delivered in 1837.
6   Pierre-Joseph Proudhon, *What Is Property? or, An Inquiry into the Principle of Right and of Government*, first published in 1840.

labor within the last few decades far exceeds normal demand. But what are normal demands to an abnormal institution? The only demand that property recognizes is its own gluttonous appetite for greater wealth; because wealth means power; the power to subdue, to crush, to exploit, the power to enslave, to outrage, to degrade. America is particularly boastful of her great power, her enormous national wealth. Poor America, of what avail is all her wealth, if the individuals comprising the nation are wretchedly poor? If they live in squalor, in filth, in crime, with hope and joy gone, a homeless, soilless army of human prey.

It is generally conceded that unless the returns of any business venture exceed the cost, bankruptcy is inevitable. But those engaged in the business of producing wealth have not yet learned even this simple lesson. Every year the cost of production in human life is growing larger (50,000 killed, 100,000 wounded in America last year); the returns to the masses, who help to create wealth, are ever getting smaller. Yet America continues to be blind to the inevitable bankruptcy of our business of production. Nor is this the only crime of the latter. Still more fatal is the crime of turning the producer into a mere particle of a machine, with less, will and decision than his master of steel, and iron. Man is being robbed not merely of the products of his labor, but of the power of free initiative, of originality, and the interest in, or desire for, the things he is making.

Real wealth consists in things of utility and beauty, in things that help to create strong, beautiful bodies and surroundings inspiring to live in. But if man is doomed to wind cotton around a spool, or dig coal, or build roads for thirty years of his life, there can be no talk of wealth. What he gives to the world is only gray and hideous things, reflecting a dull and hideous existence,—too weak to live, too cowardly to die. Strange to say, there are people who extol this deadening method of centralized production as the proudest achievement of our age. They fail utterly to realize that if we are to continue in machine subserviency, our slavery is more complete than was our bondage to the King. They do not want to know that centralization is not only the death-knell of liberty, but also of health and beauty, of art and science, all these being impossible in a clock-like, mechanical atmosphere.

Anarchism cannot but repudiate such a method of production: its goal is the freest possible expression of all the latent powers of the individual. Oscar Wilde defines a perfect personality as "one who develops under perfect conditions, who is not wounded, maimed, or in danger."[7] A perfect personality, then, is only possible in a state of society where man is free to choose the mode of work, the conditions of work, and the freedom to work. One to whom the making of a table, the building of a house, or the tilling of the soil, is what the painting is to the artist and the discovery to the scientist,—the result of inspiration, of intense longing, and deep interest in work as a creative force. That being the ideal of Anarchism, its economic

7   Oscar Wilde, "The Soul of Man Under Socialism," first published in 1891.

arrangements must consist of voluntary productive and distributive associations, gradually developing into free communism, as the best means of producing with the least waste of human energy. Anarchism, however, also recognizes the right of the individual, or numbers of individuals, to arrange at all times for other forms of work, in harmony with their tastes and desires.

Such free display of human energy being possible only under complete individual and social freedom, Anarchism directs its forces against the third and greatest foe of all social equality; namely, the State, organized authority, or statutory law,—the dominion of human conduct.

Just as religion has fettered the human mind, and as property, or the monopoly of things, has subdued and stifled man's needs, so has the State enslaved his spirit, dictating every phase of conduct. "All government in essence," says Emerson, "is tyranny." It matters not whether it is government by divine right or majority rule. In every instance its aim is the absolute subordination of the individual.

Referring to the American government, the greatest American Anarchist, David Thoreau, said: "Government, what is it but a tradition, though a recent one, endeavoring to transmit itself unimpaired to posterity, but each instant losing its integrity; it has not the vitality and force of a single living man. [...] Law never made man a whit more just; and by means of their respect for it, even the well-disposed are daily made agents of injustice."[8]

Indeed, the keynote of government is injustice. With the arrogance and self-sufficiency of the King who could do no wrong, governments ordain, judge, condemn, and punish the most insignificant offenses, while maintaining themselves by the greatest of all offenses, the annihilation of individual liberty. Thus Ouida is right when she maintains that "the State only aims at instilling those qualities in its public by which its demands are obeyed, and its exchequer is filled. Its highest attainment is the reduction of mankind to clockwork. In its atmosphere all those finer and more delicate liberties, which require treatment and spacious expansion, inevitably dry up and perish. The State requires a taxpaying machine in which there is no hitch, an exchequer in which there is never a deficit, and a public, monotonous, obedient, colorless, spiritless, moving humbly like a flock of sheep along a straight high road between two walls."[9]

Yet even a flock of sheep would resist the chicanery of the State, if it were not for the corruptive, tyrannical, and oppressive methods it employs to serve its purposes. Therefore Bakunin repudiates the State as synonymous with the surrender of the liberty of the individual or small minorities,—the destruction of social relationship, the curtailment, or complete denial even, of life itself, for its own aggrandizement.

---

8   Henry David Thoreau, "Civil Disobedience," first published in 1849.
9   Ouida was the pseudonym of the English novelist Maria Louise Ramé (1839–1908) who published more than forty novels during her career.

The State is the altar of political freedom and, like the religious altar, it is maintained for the purpose of human sacrifice.

In fact, there is hardly a modern thinker who does not agree that government, organized authority, or the State, is necessary *only* to maintain or protect property and monopoly. It has proven efficient in that function only.

Even George Bernard Shaw, who hopes for the miraculous from the State under Fabianism, nevertheless admits that "it is at present a huge machine for robbing and slave-driving of the poor by brute force."[10] This being the case, it is hard to see why the clever prefacer wishes to uphold the State after poverty shall have ceased to exist.

Unfortunately there are still a number of people who continue in the fatal belief that government rests on natural laws, that it maintains social order and harmony, that it diminishes crime, and that it prevents the lazy man from fleecing his fellows. I shall therefore examine these contentions.

A natural law is that factor in man which asserts itself freely and spontaneously without any external force, in harmony with the requirements of nature. For instance, the demand for nutrition, for sex gratification, for light, air, and exercise, is a natural law. But its expression needs not the machinery of government, needs not the club, the gun, the handcuff, or the prison. To obey such laws, if we may call it obedience, requires only spontaneity and free opportunity. That governments do not maintain themselves through such harmonious factors is proven by the terrible array of violence, force, and coercion all governments use in order to live. Thus Blackstone is right when he says, "Human laws are invalid, because they are contrary to the laws of nature."

Unless it be the order of Warsaw after the slaughter of thousands of people, it is difficult to ascribe to governments any capacity for order or social harmony. Order derived through submission and maintained by terror is not much of a safe guaranty; yet that is the only "order" that governments have ever maintained. True social harmony grows naturally out of solidarity of interests. In a society where those who always work never have anything, while those who never work enjoy everything, solidarity of interests is non-existent; hence social harmony is but a myth. The only way organized authority meets this grave situation is by extending still greater privileges to those who have already monopolized the earth, and by still further enslaving the disinherited masses. Thus the entire arsenal of government—laws, police, soldiers, the courts, legislatures, prisons,—is strenuously engaged in "harmonizing" the most antagonistic elements in society.

The most absurd apology for authority and law is that they serve to diminish crime. Aside from the fact that the State is itself the greatest criminal, breaking every written and natural law, stealing in the form of taxes, killing in the form of war and capital punishment, it has come to an absolute standstill in coping with crime. It has

---

10   George Bernard Shaw, "The Impossibilities of Anarchism," first published in 1895.

failed utterly to destroy or even minimize the horrible scourge of its own creation.

Crime is naught but misdirected energy. So long as every institution of today, economic, political, social, and moral, conspires to misdirect human energy into wrong channels; so long as most people are out of place doing the things they hate to do, living a life they loathe to live, crime will be inevitable, and all the laws on the statutes can only increase, but never do away with, crime. What does society, as it exists today, know of the process of despair, the poverty, the horrors, the fearful struggle the human soul must pass on its way to crime and degradation. Who that knows this terrible process can fail to see the truth in these words of Peter Kropotkin:

"Those who will hold the balance between the benefits thus attributed to law and punishment and the degrading effect of the latter on humanity; those who will estimate the torrent of depravity poured abroad in human society by the informer, favored by the Judge even, and paid for in clinking cash by governments, under the pretext of aiding to unmask crime; those who will go within prison walls and there see what human beings become when deprived of liberty, when subjected to the care of brutal keepers, to coarse, cruel words, to a thousand stinging, piercing humiliations, will agree with us that the entire apparatus of prison and punishment is an abomination which ought to be brought to an end."

The deterrent influence of law on the lazy man is too absurd to merit consideration. If society were only relieved of the waste and expense of keeping a lazy class, and the equally great expense of the paraphernalia of protection this lazy class requires, the social tables would contain an abundance for all, including even the occasional lazy individual. Besides, it is well to consider that laziness results either from special privileges, or physical and mental abnormalities. Our present insane system of production fosters both, and the most astounding phenomenon is that people should want to work at all now. Anarchism aims to strip labor of its deadening, dulling aspect, of its gloom and compulsion. It aims to make work an instrument of joy, of strength, of color, of real harmony, so that the poorest sort of a man should find in work both recreation and hope.

To achieve such an arrangement of life, government, with its unjust, arbitrary, repressive measures, must be done away with. At best it has but imposed one single mode of life upon all, without regard to individual and social variations and needs. In destroying government and statutory laws, Anarchism proposes to rescue the self-respect and independence of the individual from all restraint and invasion by authority. Only in freedom can man grow to his full stature. Only in freedom will he learn to think and move, and give the very best in him. Only in freedom will he realize the true force of the social bonds which knit men together, and which are the true foundation of a normal social life.

But what about human nature? Can it be changed? And if not, will it endure under Anarchism?

Poor human nature, what horrible crimes have been committed in thy name! Every fool, from king to policeman, from the flatheaded parson to the visionless dabbler in science, presumes to speak authoritatively of human nature. The greater the mental charlatan, the more definite his insistence on the wickedness and weaknesses of human nature. Yet, how can anyone speak of it today, with every soul in a prison, with every heart fettered, wounded, and maimed?

John Burroughs has stated that experimental study of animals in captivity is absolutely useless.[11] Their character, their habits, their appetites undergo a complete transformation when torn from their soil in field and forest. With human nature caged in a narrow space, whipped daily into submission, how can we speak of its potentialities?

Freedom, expansion, opportunity, and, above all, peace and repose, alone can teach us the real dominant factors of human nature and all its wonderful possibilities.

Anarchism, then, really stands for the liberation of the human mind from the dominion of religion; the liberation of the human body from the dominion of property; liberation from the shackles and restraint of government. Anarchism stands for a social order based on the free grouping of individuals for the purpose of producing real social wealth; an order that will guarantee to every human being free access to the earth and full enjoyment of the necessities of life, according to individual desires, tastes, and inclinations.

This is not a wild fancy or an aberration of the mind. It is the conclusion arrived at by hosts of intellectual men and women the world over; a conclusion resulting from the close and studious observation of the tendencies of modern society: individual liberty and economic equality, the twin forces for the birth of what is fine and true in man.

As to methods. Anarchism is not, as some may suppose, a theory of the future to be realized through divine inspiration. It is a living force in the affairs of our life, constantly creating new conditions. The methods of Anarchism therefore do not comprise an iron-clad program to be carried out under all circumstances. Methods must grow out of the economic needs of each place and clime, and of the intellectual and temperamental requirements of the individual. The serene, calm character of a Tolstoy will wish different methods for social reconstruction than the intense, overflowing personality of a Michael Bakunin or a Peter Kropotkin. Equally so it must be apparent that the economic and political needs of Russia will dictate more drastic measures than would England or America. Anarchism does not stand for military drill and uniformity; it does, however, stand for the spirit of revolt, in whatever form, against everything that hinders human growth. All Anarchists agree in that, as they

---

11   John Burroughs (1837–1921) was an American naturalist who advocated for a realistic rather than fantastical depiction of the natural world.

also agree in their opposition to the political machinery as a means of bringing about the great social change.

"All voting," says Thoreau, "is a sort of gaming, like checkers, or backgammon [...], a playing with right and wrong; [...] its obligation [...] never exceeds that of expediency. Even voting for the right thing is doing nothing for it. [...] A wise man will not leave the right to the mercy of chance, nor wish it to prevail through the power of the majority."[12] A close examination of the machinery of politics and its achievements will bear out the logic of Thoreau.

What does the history of parliamentarism show? Nothing but failure and defeat, not even a single reform to ameliorate the economic and social stress of the people. Laws have been passed and enactments, made for the improvement and protection of labor. Thus it was proven only last year that Illinois, with the most rigid laws for mine protection, had the greatest mine disasters. In States where child labor laws prevail, child exploitation is at its highest, and though with us, the workers enjoy full political opportunities, capitalism has reached the most brazen zenith.

Even were the workers able to have their own representatives, for which our good Socialist politicians are clamoring, what chances are there for their honesty and good faith? One has but to bear in mind the process of politics to realize that its path of good intentions is full of pitfalls: wire-pulling, intriguing, flattering, lying, cheating; in fact, chicanery of every description, whereby the political aspirant can achieve success. Added to that is a complete demoralization of character and conviction, until nothing is left that would make one hope for anything from such a human derelict. Time and time again the people were foolish enough to trust, believe, and support with their last farthing aspiring politicians, only to find themselves betrayed and cheated.

It may be claimed that men of integrity would not become corrupt in the political grinding mill. Perhaps not; but such men would be absolutely helpless to exert the slightest influence in behalf of labor, as indeed has been shown in numerous instances. The State is the economic master of its servants. Good men, if such there be, would either remain true to their political faith and lose their economic support, or they would cling to their economic master and be utterly unable to do the slightest good. The political arena leaves one no alternative, one must either be a dunce or a rogue.

The political superstition is still holding sway over the hearts and minds of the masses, but the true lovers of liberty will have no more to do with it. Instead, they believe with Stirner that man has as much liberty as he is willing to take. Anarchism therefore stands for direct action, the open defiance of, and resistance to, all laws and restrictions, economic, social, and moral. But defiance and resistance are illegal. Therein lies the salvation of man. Everything illegal necessitates integrity,

---

12   Henry David Thoreau, "Civil Disobedience." Ellipses added to Goldman's citation.

self-reliance, and courage. In short, it calls for free, independent spirits, for "men who are men, and who have a bone in their backs which you cannot pass your hand through."

Universal suffrage itself owes its existence to direct action. If not for the spirit of rebellion, of the defiance on the part of the American revolutionary fathers, their posterity would still wear the King's coat. If not for the direct action of a John Brown and his comrades, America would still trade in the flesh of the black man. True, the trade in white flesh is still going on; but that, too, will have to be abolished by direct action. Trade-unionism, the economic arena of the modern gladiator, owes its existence to direct action. It is but recently that law and government have attempted to crush the trade-union movement, and condemned the exponents of man's right to organize to prison as conspirators. Had they sought to assert their cause through begging, pleading, and compromise, trade-unionism would today be a negligible quantity. In France, in Spain, in Italy, in Russia, nay even in England (witness the growing rebellion of English labor unions), direct, revolutionary, economic action has become so strong a force in the battle for industrial liberty as to make the world realize the tremendous importance of labor's power. The General Strike, the supreme expression of the economic consciousness of the workers, was ridiculed in America but a short time ago. Today every great strike, in order to win, must realize the importance of the solidaric general protest.

Direct action, having proven effective along economic lines, is equally potent in the environment of the individual. There a hundred forces encroach upon his being, and only persistent resistance to them will finally set him free. Direct action against the authority in the shop, direct action against the authority of the law, direct action against the invasive, meddlesome authority of our moral code, is the logical, consistent method of Anarchism.

Will it not lead to a revolution? Indeed, it will. No real social change has ever come about without a revolution. People are either not familiar with their history, or they have not yet learned that revolution is but thought carried into action.

Anarchism, the great leaven of thought, is today permeating every phase of human endeavor. Science, art, literature, the drama, the effort for economic betterment, in fact every individual and social opposition to the existing disorder of things, is illumined by the spiritual light of Anarchism. It is the philosophy of the sovereignty of the individual. It is the theory of social harmony. It is the great, surging, living truth that is reconstructing the world, and that will usher in the Dawn.

THE PSYCHOLOGY OF POLITICAL VIOLENCE

T O ANALYZE THE psychology of political violence is not only extremely difficult, but also very dangerous. If such acts are treated with understanding, one is immediately accused of eulogizing them. If, on the other hand, human sympathy is expressed with the *Attentäter*[13] one risks being considered a possible accomplice. Yet it is only intelligence and sympathy that can bring us closer to the source of human suffering, and teach us the ultimate way out of it.

The primitive man, ignorant of natural forces, dreaded their approach, hiding from the perils they threatened. As man learned to understand Nature's phenomena, he realized that though these may destroy life and cause great loss, they also bring relief. To the earnest student it must be apparent that the accumulated forces in our social and economic life, culminating in a political act of violence, are similar to the terrors of the atmosphere, manifested in storm and lightning.

To thoroughly appreciate the truth of this view, one must feel intensely the indignity of our social wrongs; one's very being must throb with the pain, the sorrow, the despair millions of people are daily made to endure. Indeed, unless we have become a part of humanity, we cannot even faintly understand the just indignation that accumulates in a human soul, the burning, surging passion that makes the storm inevitable.

The ignorant mass looks upon the man who makes a violent protest against our social and economic iniquities as upon a wild beast, a cruel, heartless monster, whose joy it is to destroy life and bathe in blood; or at best, as upon an irresponsible lunatic. Yet nothing is further from the truth. As a matter of fact, those who have studied the character and personality of these men, or who have come in close contact with them, are agreed that it is their supersensitiveness to the wrong and injustice surrounding them which compels them to pay the toll of our social crimes. The most noted writers and poets, discussing the psychology of political offenders, have paid them the highest tribute. Could anyone assume that these men had advised violence, or even approved of the acts? Certainly not. Theirs was the attitude of the social student, of the man who knows that beyond every violent act there is a vital cause.

Bjørnstjerne Bjørnson, in the second part of *Beyond Human Power,* emphasizes

---

13   German word for political assassin, used here to refer to any individual committed to violent action for a political cause.

the fact that it is among the Anarchists that we must look for the modern martyrs who pay for their faith with their blood, and who welcome death with a smile, because they believe, as truly as Christ did, that their martyrdom will redeem humanity.[14]

François Coppée, the French novelist, thus expresses himself regarding the psychology of the *Attentäter*[15]:

"The reading of the details of Vaillant's execution left me in a thoughtful mood. I imagined him expanding his chest under the ropes, marching with firm step, stiffening his will, concentrating all his energy, and, with eyes fixed upon the knife, hurling finally at society his cry of malediction. And, in spite of me, another spectacle rose suddenly before my mind. I saw a group of men and women pressing against each other in the middle of the oblong arena of the circus, under the gaze of thousands of eyes, while from all the steps of the immense amphitheatre went up the terrible cry, *Ad leones!* and, below, the opening cages of the wild beasts.

"I did not believe the execution would take place. In the first place, no victim had been struck with death, and it had long been the custom not to punish an abortive crime with the last degree of severity. Then, this crime, however terrible in intention, was disinterested, born of an abstract idea. The man's past, his abandoned childhood, his life of hardship, pleaded also in his favor. In the independent press generous voices were raised in his behalf, very loud and eloquent. 'A purely literary current of opinion' some have said, with no little scorn. *It is, on the contrary, an honor to the men of art and thought to have expressed once more their disgust at the scaffold.*"

Again Zola, in *Germinal* and *Paris*, describes the tenderness and kindness, the deep sympathy with human suffering, of these men who close the chapter of their lives with a violent outbreak against our system.[16]

Last, but not least, the man who probably better than anyone else understands the psychology of the *Attentäter* is M. Hamon, the author of the brilliant work *La psychologie du militaire professionnel*, who has arrived at these suggestive conclusions:

"The positive method confirmed by the rational method enables us to establish an ideal type of Anarchist, whose mentality is the aggregate of common psychic characteristics. Every Anarchist partakes sufficiently of this ideal type to make it possible to differentiate him from other men. The typical Anarchist, then, may be defined as follows: A man perceptible by the spirit of revolt under one or more of its forms,—opposition, investigation, criticism, innovation,—endowed with a strong love of liberty, egoistic or individualistic, and possessed of great curiosity, a keen desire to know. These traits are supplemented by an ardent love of others, a highly

---

14 Bjørnstjerne Martinius Bjørnson (1832–1910), Norwegian author awarded the 1903 Nobel Prize in Literature.
15 François Coppée, (1842–1908), French literary author.
16 Émile Zola (1814–1902), French novelist, critic, and social activist.

developed moral sensitiveness, a profound sentiment of justice, and imbued with missionary zeal.[17]"

To the above characteristics, says Alvan F. Sanborn, must be added these sterling qualities: "a rare love of animals, surpassing sweetness in all the ordinary relations of life, exceptional sobriety of demeanor, frugality and regularity, austerity, even, of living, and courage beyond compare."[18]

"There is a truism that the man in the street seems always to forget, when he is abusing the Anarchists, or whatever party happens to be his *bête noire* for the moment, as the cause of some outrage just perpetrated. This indisputable fact is that homicidal outrages have, from time immemorial, been the reply of goaded and desperate classes, and goaded and desperate individuals, to wrongs from their fellowmen, which they felt to be intolerable. Such acts are the violent recoil from violence, whether aggressive or repressive; they are the last desperate struggle of outraged and exasperated human nature for breathing space and life. And their cause lies not in any special conviction, but in the depths of that human nature itself. The whole course of history, political and social, is strewn with evidence of this fact. To go no further, take the three most notorious examples of political parties goaded into violence during the last fifty years: the Mazzinians in Italy, the Fenians in Ireland, and the Terrorists in Russia. Were these people Anarchists? No. Did they all three even hold the same political opinions? No. The Mazzinians were Republicans, the Fenians political separatists, the Russians Social Democrats or Constitutionalists. But all were driven by desperate circumstances into this terrible form of revolt. And when we turn from parties to individuals who have acted in like manner, we stand appalled by the number of humane beings goaded and driven by sheer desperation into conduct obviously violently opposed to their social instincts.

"Now that Anarchism has become a living force in society, such deeds have been sometimes committed by Anarchists, as well as by others. For no new faith, even the most essentially peaceable and humane the mind of man has yet accepted, but at its first coming has brought upon earth not peace, but a sword; not because of anything violent or anti-social in the doctrine itself; simply because of the ferment any new and creative idea excites in men's minds, whether they accept or reject it. And a conception of Anarchism, which, on one hand, threatens every vested interest, and, on the other, holds out a vision of a free and noble life to be won by a struggle against existing wrongs, is certain to rouse the fiercest opposition, and bring the

---

17   Augustin Frédéric Adolphe Hamon (1862–1945), French political writer; he published *La psychologie du militaire professionnel* in 1894.
18   Alvan Francis Sanborn (1866–1966), American journalist and author who spent much of his life in France. The list of qualities is a citation from Sanborn's *Paris and the Social Revolution. A Study of the Revolutionary Elements in the Various Classes of Parisian Society* (1905).

whole repressive force of ancient evil into violent contact with the tumultuous out-
burst of a new hope.

"Under miserable conditions of life, any vision of the possibility of better things
makes the present misery more intolerable, and spurs those who suffer to the most
energetic struggles to improve their lot, and if these struggles only immediately
result in sharper misery, the outcome is sheer desperation. In our present society,
for instance, an exploited wage worker, who catches a glimpse of what work and life
might and ought to be, finds the toilsome routine and the squalor of his existence
almost intolerable; and even when he has the resolution and courage to continue
steadily working his best, and waiting until new ideas have so permeated society
as to pave the way for better times, the mere fact that he has such ideas and tries to
spread them, brings him into difficulties with his employers. How many thousands
of Socialists, and above all Anarchists, have lost work and even the chance of work,
solely on the ground of their opinions. It is only the specially gifted craftsman, who, if
he be a zealous propagandist, can hope to retain permanent employment. And what
happens to a man with his brain working actively with a ferment of new ideas, with
a vision before his eyes of a new hope dawning for toiling and agonizing men, with
the knowledge that his suffering and that of his fellows in misery is not caused by the
cruelty of fate, but by the injustice of other human beings,—what happens to such
a man when he sees those dear to him starving, when he himself is starved? Some
natures in such a plight, and those by no means the least social or the least sensitive,
will become violent, and will even feel that their violence is social and not anti-social,
that in striking when and how they can, they are striking, not for themselves, but
for human nature, outraged and despoiled in their persons and in those of their
fellow sufferers. And are we, who ourselves are not in this horrible predicament,
to stand by and coldly condemn these piteous victims of the Furies and Fates? Are
we to decry as miscreants these human beings who act with heroic self-devotion,
sacrificing their lives in protest, where less social and less energetic natures would
lie down and grovel in abject submission to injustice and wrong? Are we to join the
ignorant and brutal outcry which stigmatizes such men as monsters of wickedness,
gratuitously running amuck in a harmonious and innocently peaceful society? No!
We hate murder with a hatred that may seem absurdly exaggerated to apologists for
Matabele massacres, to callous acquiescers in hangings and bombardments, but we
decline in such cases of homicide, or attempted homicide, as those of which we are
treating, to be guilty of the cruel injustice of flinging the whole responsibility of the
deed upon the immediate perpetrator.[19] The guilt of these homicides lies upon every
man and woman who, intentionally or by cold indifference, helps to keep up social

---

19   Refers to the massacre of Matabele people of the Ndebele kingdom in Southern Africa by
the British South Africa Company in the 1890s, which led to the establishment of Rhodesia
under British rule (now Zimbabwe).

conditions that drive human beings to despair. The man who flings his whole life into the attempt, at the cost of his own life, to protest against the wrongs of his fellow men, is a saint compared to the active and passive upholders of cruelty and injustice, even if his protest destroy other lives besides his own. Let him who is without sin in society cast the first stone at such an one."[20]

That every act of political violence should nowadays be attributed to Anarchists is not at all surprising. Yet it is a fact known to almost everyone familiar with the Anarchist movement that a great number of acts, for which Anarchists had to suffer, either originated with the capitalist press or were instigated, if not directly perpetrated, by the police.

For a number of years acts of violence had been committed in Spain, for which the Anarchists were held responsible, hounded like wild beasts, and thrown into prison. Later it was disclosed that the perpetrators of these acts were not Anarchists, but members of the police department. The scandal became so widespread that the conservative Spanish papers demanded the apprehension and punishment of the gang-leader, Juan Rull, who was subsequently condemned to death and executed. The sensational evidence, brought to light during the trial, forced Police Inspector Momento to exonerate completely the Anarchists from any connection with the acts committed during a long period. This resulted in the dismissal of a number of police officials, among them Inspector Tressols, who, in revenge, disclosed the fact that behind the gang of police bomb throwers were others of far higher position, who provided them with funds and protected them.

This is one of the many striking examples of how Anarchist conspiracies are manufactured.

That the American police can perjure themselves with the same ease, that they are just as merciless, just as brutal and cunning as their European colleagues, has been proven on more than one occasion. We need only recall the tragedy of the eleventh of November, 1887, known as the Haymarket Riot.[21]

No one who is at all familiar with the case can possibly doubt that the Anarchists, judicially murdered in Chicago, died as victims of a lying, bloodthirsty press and of a cruel police conspiracy. Has not Judge Gary himself said: "Not because you have caused the Haymarket bomb, but because you are Anarchists, you are on trial."

The impartial and thorough analysis by Governor Altgeld of that blotch on the American escutcheon verified the brutal frankness of Judge Gary. It was this that induced Altgeld to pardon the three Anarchists, thereby earning the lasting esteem of every liberty-loving man and woman in the world.

---

20   From a pamphlet published by the Freedom Group of London.
21   The Haymarket riot refers to the aftermath of a bombing at a labor demonstration on May 4, 1886, in Chicago, United States, which claimed the lives of several policemen and civilians and led to the trial and execution of several anarchists for conspiracy. It is often considered a milestone in the labor movement.

When we approach the tragedy of September 6, 1901, we are confronted by one of the most striking examples of how little social theories are responsible for an act of political violence.[22] "Leon Czolgosz, an Anarchist, incited to commit the act by Emma Goldman." To be sure, has she not incited violence even before her birth, and will she not continue to do so beyond death? Everything is possible with the Anarchists.

Today, even, nine years after the tragedy, after it was proven a hundred times that Emma Goldman had nothing to do with the event, that no evidence whatsoever exists to indicate that Czolgosz ever called himself an Anarchist, we are confronted with the same lie, fabricated by the police and perpetuated by the press. No living soul ever heard Czolgosz make that statement, nor is there a single written word to prove that the boy ever breathed the accusation. Nothing but ignorance and insane hysteria, which have never yet been able to solve the simplest problem of cause and effect.

The President of a free Republic killed! What else can be the cause, except that the *Attentäter* must have been insane, or that he was incited to the act.

A free Republic! How a myth will maintain itself, how it will continue to deceive, to dupe, and blind even the comparatively intelligent to its monstrous absurdities. A free Republic! And yet within a little over thirty years a small band of parasites have successfully robbed the American people, and trampled upon the fundamental principles, laid down by the fathers of this country, guaranteeing to every man, woman, and child "life, liberty, and the pursuit of happiness." For thirty years they have been increasing their wealth and power at the expense of the vast mass of workers, thereby enlarging the army of the unemployed, the hungry, homeless, and friendless portion of humanity, who are tramping the country from east to west, from north to south, in a vain search for work. For many years the home has been left to the care of the little ones, while the parents are exhausting their life and strength for a mere pittance. For thirty years the sturdy sons of America have been sacrificed on the battlefield of industrial war, and the daughters outraged in corrupt factory surroundings. For long and weary years this process of undermining the nation's health, vigor, and pride, without much protest from the disinherited and oppressed, has been going on. Maddened by success and victory, the money powers of this "free land of ours" became more and more audacious in their heartless, cruel efforts to compete with the rotten and decayed European tyrannies for supremacy of power.

In vain did a lying press repudiate Leon Czolgosz as a foreigner. The boy was a product of our own free American soil, that lulled him to sleep with,

> My country, 'tis of thee,
> Sweet land of liberty.

---

22   Day of the assassination of U.S. President William McKinley.

Who can tell how many times this American child had gloried in the celebration of the Fourth of July, or of Decoration Day, when he faithfully honored the Nation's dead? Who knows but that he, too, was willing to "fight for his country and die for her liberty," until it dawned upon him that those he belonged to have no country, because they have been robbed of all that they have produced; until he realized that the liberty and independence of his youthful dreams were but a farce. Poor Leon Czolgosz, your crime consisted of too sensitive a social consciousness. Unlike your idealless and brainless American brothers, your ideals soared above the belly and the bank account. No wonder you impressed the one human being among all the infuriated mob at your trial—a newspaper woman—as a visionary, totally oblivious to your surroundings. Your large, dreamy eyes must have beheld a new and glorious dawn.

Now, to a recent instance of police-manufactured Anarchist plots. In that bloodstained city Chicago, the life of Chief of Police Shippy was attempted by a young man named Averbuch. Immediately the cry was sent to the four corners of the world that Averbuch was an Anarchist, and that the Anarchists were responsible for the act. Everyone who was at all known to entertain Anarchist ideas was closely watched, a number of people arrested, the library of an Anarchist group confiscated, and all meetings made impossible. It goes without saying that, as on various previous occasions, I must needs be held responsible for the act. Evidently the American police credit me with occult powers. I did not know Averbuch; in fact, had never before heard his name, and the only way I could have possibly "conspired" with him was in my astral body. But, then, the police are not concerned with logic or justice. What they seek is a target, to mask their absolute ignorance of the cause, of the psychology of a political act. Was Averbuch an Anarchist? There is no positive proof of it. He had been but three months in the country, did not know the language, and, as far as I could ascertain, was quite unknown to the Anarchists of Chicago.

What led to his act? Averbuch, like most young Russian immigrants, undoubtedly believed in the mythical liberty of America. He received his first baptism by the policeman's club during the brutal dispersement of the unemployed parade. He further experienced American equality and opportunity in the vain efforts to find an economic master. In short, a three months' sojourn in the glorious land brought him face to face with the fact that the disinherited are in the same position the world over. In his native land he probably learned that necessity knows no law—here was no difference between a Russian and an American policeman.

The question to the intelligent social student is not whether the acts of Czolgosz or Averbuch were practical, any more than whether the thunderstorm is practical. The thing that will inevitably impress itself on the thinking and feeling man and woman is that the sight of brutal clubbing of innocent victims in a so-called free Republic, and the degrading, soul-destroying economic struggle, furnish the spark that kindles the dynamic force in the overwrought, outraged souls of men like Czolgosz or

Averbuch. No amount of persecution, of hounding, of repression, can stay this social phenomenon.

But, it is often asked, have not acknowledged Anarchists committed acts of violence? Certainly they have, always however ready to shoulder the responsibility. My contention is that they were impelled, not by the teachings of Anarchism, but by the tremendous pressure of conditions, making life unbearable to their sensitive natures. Obviously, Anarchism, or any other social theory, making man a conscious social unit, will act as a leaven for rebellion. This is not a mere assertion, but a fact verified by all experience. A close examination of the circumstances bearing upon this question will further clarify my position.

Let us consider some of the most important Anarchist acts within the last two decades. Strange as it may seem, one of the most significant deeds of political violence occurred here in America, in connection with the Homestead strike of 1892.

During that memorable time the Carnegie Steel Company organized a conspiracy to crush the Amalgamated Association of Iron and Steel Workers. Henry Clay Frick, then Chairman of the Company, was entrusted with that democratic task. He lost no time in carrying out the policy of breaking the Union, the policy which he had so successfully practiced during his reign of terror in the coke regions. Secretly, and while peace negotiations were being purposely prolonged, Frick supervised the military preparations, the fortification of the Homestead Steel Works, the erection of a high board fence, capped with barbed wire and provided with loopholes for sharpshooters. And then, in the dead of night, he attempted to smuggle his army of hired Pinkerton thugs into Homestead, which act precipitated the terrible carnage of the steel workers. Not content with the death of eleven victims, killed in the Pinkerton skirmish, Henry Clay Frick, good Christian and free American, straightway began the hounding down of the helpless wives and orphans, by ordering them out of the wretched Company houses.

The whole country was aroused over these inhuman outrages. Hundreds of voices were raised in protest, calling on Frick to desist, not to go too far. Yes, hundreds of people protested,—as one objects to annoying flies. Only one there was who actively responded to the outrage at Homestead,—Alexander Berkman. Yes, he was an Anarchist. He gloried in that fact, because it was the only force that made the discord between his spiritual longing and the world without at all bearable. Yet not Anarchism, as such, but the brutal slaughter of the eleven steel workers was the urge for Alexander Berkman's act, his attempt on the life of Henry Clay Frick.

The record of European acts of political violence affords numerous and striking instances of the influence of environment upon sensitive human beings.

The court speech of Vaillant, who, in 1894, exploded a bomb in the Paris Chamber of Deputies, strikes the true keynote of the psychology of such acts:[23]

---

23   Auguste Vaillant (1861–1894), French anarchist who committed a bomb attack on the

"Gentlemen, in a few minutes you are to deal your blow, but in receiving your verdict I shall have at least the satisfaction of having wounded the existing society, that cursed society in which one may see a single man spending, uselessly, enough to feed thousands of families; an infamous society which permits a few individuals to monopolize all the social wealth, while there are hundreds of thousands of unfortunates who have not even the bread that is not refused to dogs, and while entire families are committing suicide for want of the necessities of life.

"Ah, gentlemen, if the governing classes could go down among the unfortunates! But no, they prefer to remain deaf to their appeals. It seems that a fatality impels them, like the royalty of the eighteenth century, toward the precipice which will engulf them, for woe be to those who remain deaf to the cries of the starving, woe to those who, believing themselves of superior essence, assume the right to exploit those beneath them! There comes a time when the people no longer reason; they rise like a hurricane, and pass away like a torrent. Then we see bleeding heads impaled on pikes.

"Among the exploited, gentlemen, there are two classes of individuals. Those of one class, not realizing what they are and what they might be, take life as it comes, believe that they are born to be slaves, and content themselves with the little that is given them in exchange for their labor. But there are others, on the contrary, who think, who study, and who, looking about them, discover social iniquities. Is it their fault if they see clearly and suffer at seeing others suffer? Then they throw themselves into the struggle, and make themselves the bearers of the popular claims.

"Gentlemen, I am one of these last. Wherever I have gone, I have seen unfortunates bent beneath the yoke of capital. Everywhere I have seen the same wounds causing tears of blood to flow, even in the remoter parts of the inhabited districts of South America, where I had the right to believe that he who was weary of the pains of civilization might rest in the shade of the palm trees and there study nature. Well, there even, more than elsewhere, I have seen capital come, like a vampire, to suck the last drop of blood of the unfortunate pariahs.

"Then I came back to France, where it was reserved for me to see my family suffer atrociously. This was the last drop in the cup of my sorrow. Tired of leading this life of suffering and cowardice, I carried this bomb to those who are primarily responsible for social misery.

"I am reproached with the wounds of those who were hit by my projectiles. Permit me to point out in passing that, if the bourgeois had not massacred or caused massacres during the Revolution, it is probable that they would still be under the yoke of the nobility. On the other hand, figure up the dead and wounded of Tonquin, Madagascar, Dahomey, adding thereto the thousands, yes, millions of unfortunates who die in the factories, the mines, and wherever the grinding power of capital is felt.

French Chamber of Deputies in 1893, for which he was executed in 1894.

Add also those who die of hunger, and all this with the assent of our Deputies. Beside all this, of how little weight are the reproaches now brought against me!

"It is true that one does not efface the other; but, after all, are we not acting on the defensive when we respond to the blows which we receive from above? I know very well that I shall be told that I ought to have confined myself to speech for the vindication of the people's claims. But what can you expect! It takes a loud voice to make the deaf hear. Too long have they answered our voices by imprisonment, the rope, rifle volleys. Make no mistake; the explosion of my bomb is not only the cry of the rebel Vaillant, but the cry of an entire class which vindicates its rights, and which will soon add acts to words. For, be sure of it, in vain will they pass laws. The ideas of the thinkers will not halt; just as, in the last century, all the governmental forces could not prevent the Diderots and the Voltaires from spreading emancipating ideas among the people, so all the existing governmental forces will not prevent the Reclus, the Darwins, the Spencers, the Ibsens, the Mirbeaus, from spreading the ideas of justice and liberty which will annihilate the prejudices that hold the mass in ignorance. And these ideas, welcomed by the unfortunate, will flower in acts of revolt as they have done in me, until the day when the disappearance of authority shall permit all men to organize freely according to their choice, when everyone shall be able to enjoy the product of his labor, and when those moral maladies called prejudices shall vanish, permitting human beings to live in harmony, having no other desire than to study the sciences and love their fellows.

"I conclude, gentlemen, by saying that a society in which one sees such social inequalities as we see all about us, in which we see every day suicides caused by poverty, prostitution flaring at every street corner,—a society whose principal monuments are barracks and prisons,—such a society must be transformed as soon as possible, on pain of being eliminated, and that speedily, from the human race. Hail to him who labors, by no matter what means, for this transformation! It is this idea that has guided me in my duel with authority, but as in this duel I have only wounded my adversary, it is now its turn to strike me.

"Now, gentlemen, to me it matters little what penalty you may inflict, for, looking at this assembly with the eyes of reason, I cannot help smiling to see you, atoms lost in matter, and reasoning only because you possess a prolongation of the spinal marrow, assume the right to judge one of your fellows.

"Ah! gentlemen, how little a thing is your assembly and your verdict in the history of humanity; and human history, in its turn, is likewise a very little thing in the whirlwind which bears it through immensity, and which is destined to disappear, or at least to be transformed, in order to begin again the same history and the same facts, a veritably perpetual play of cosmic forces renewing and transferring themselves forever."

Will anyone say that Vaillant was an ignorant, vicious man, or a lunatic? Was not his mind singularly clear and analytic? No wonder that the best intellectual forces of France spoke in his behalf, and signed the petition to President Carnot, asking him to commute Vaillant's death sentence.

Carnot would listen to no entreaty; he insisted on more than a pound of flesh, he wanted Vaillant's life, and then—the inevitable happened: President Carnot was killed. On the handle of the stiletto used by the *Attentäter* was engraved, significantly,

VAILLANT!

Santa Caserio was an Anarchist. He could have gotten away, saved himself; but he remained, he stood the consequences.

His reasons for the act are set forth in so simple, dignified, and childlike manner that one is reminded of the touching tribute paid Caserio by his teacher of the little village school, Ada Negri, the Italian poet, who spoke of him as a sweet, tender plant, of too fine and sensitive texture to stand the cruel strain of the world.

"Gentlemen of the Jury! I do not propose to make a defense, but only an explanation of my deed.

"Since my early youth I began to learn that present society is badly organized, so badly that every day many wretched men commit suicide, leaving women and children in the most terrible distress. Workers, by thousands, seek for work and cannot find it. Poor families beg for food and shiver with cold; they suffer the greatest misery; the little ones ask their miserable mothers for food, and the mothers cannot give it to them, because they have nothing. The few things which the home contained have already been sold or pawned. All they can do is beg alms; often they are arrested as vagabonds.

"I went away from my native place because I was frequently moved to tears at seeing little girls of eight or ten years obliged to work fifteen hours a day for the paltry pay of twenty centimes. Young women of eighteen or twenty also work fifteen hours daily, for a mockery of remuneration. And that happens not only to my fellow countrymen, but to all the workers, who sweat the whole day long for a crust of bread, while their labor produces wealth in abundance. The workers are obliged to live under the most wretched conditions, and their food consists of a little bread, a few spoonfuls of rice, and water; so by the time they are thirty or forty years old, they are exhausted, and go to die in the hospitals. Besides, in consequence of bad food and overwork, these unhappy creatures are, by hundreds, devoured by pellagra—a disease that, in my country, attacks, as the physicians say, those who are badly fed and lead a life of toil and privation.

"I have observed that there are a great many people who are hungry, and many children who suffer, whilst bread and clothes abound in the towns. I saw many and large shops full of clothing and woolen stuffs, and I also saw warehouses full of wheat and Indian corn, suitable for those who are in want. And, on the other hand, I saw thousands of people who do not work, who produce nothing and live on the labor of others; who spend every day thousands of francs for their amusement; who debauch the daughters of the workers; who own dwellings of forty or fifty rooms; twenty or thirty horses, many servants; in a word, all the pleasures of life.

"I believed in God; but when I saw so great an inequality between men, I acknowledged that it was not God who created man, but man who created God. And I discovered that those who want their property to be respected, have an interest in preaching the existence of paradise and hell, and in keeping the people in ignorance.

"Not long ago, Vaillant threw a bomb in the Chamber of Deputies, to protest against the present system of society. He killed no one, only wounded some persons; yet bourgeois justice sentenced him to death. And not satisfied with the condemnation of the guilty man, they began to pursue the Anarchists, and arrest not only those who had known Vaillant, but even those who had merely been present at any Anarchist lecture.

"The government did not think of their wives and children. It did not consider that the men kept in prison were not the only ones who suffered, and that their little ones cried for bread. Bourgeois justice did not trouble itself about these innocent ones, who do not yet know what society is. It is no fault of theirs that their fathers are in prison; they only want to eat.

"The government went on searching private houses, opening private letters, forbidding lectures and meetings, and practicing the most infamous oppressions against us. Even now, hundreds of Anarchists are arrested for having written an article in a newspaper, or for having expressed an opinion in public.

"Gentlemen of the Jury, you are representatives of bourgeois society. If you want my head, take it; but do not believe that in so doing you will stop the Anarchist propaganda. Take care, for men reap what they have sown."

During a religious procession in 1896, at Barcelona, a bomb was thrown. Immediately three hundred men and women were arrested. Some were Anarchists, but the majority were trade-unionists and Socialists. They were thrown into that terrible bastille Montjuich, and subjected to most horrible tortures. After a number had been killed, or had gone insane, their cases were taken up by the liberal press of Europe, resulting in the release of a few survivors.

The man primarily responsible for this revival of the Inquisition was Canovas del Castillo, Prime Minister of Spain. It was he who ordered the torturing of the victims, their flesh burned, their bones crushed, their tongues cut out. Practiced in the art of brutality during his regime in Cuba, Canovas remained absolutely deaf to the appeals and protests of the awakened civilized conscience.

In 1897 Canovas del Castillo was shot to death by a young Italian, Angiolillo.[24]

24 See note 3 above.

The latter was an editor in his native land, and his bold utterances soon attracted the attention of the authorities. Persecution began, and Angiolillo fled from Italy to Spain, thence to France and Belgium, finally settling in England. While there he found employment as a compositor, and immediately became the friend of all his colleagues. One of the latter thus described Angiolillo: "His appearance suggested the journalist rather than the disciple of Guttenberg. His delicate hands, moreover, betrayed the fact that he had not grown up at the 'case.' With his handsome frank face, his soft dark hair, his alert expression, he looked the very type of the vivacious Southerner. Angiolillo spoke Italian, Spanish, and French, but no English; the little French I knew was not sufficient to carry on a prolonged conversation. However, Angiolillo soon began to acquire the English idiom; he learned rapidly, playfully, and it was not long until he became very popular with his fellow compositors. His distinguished and yet modest manner, and his consideration towards his colleagues, won him the hearts of all the boys."

Angiolillo soon became familiar with the detailed accounts in the press. He read of the great wave of human sympathy with the helpless victims at Montjuich. On Trafalgar Square he saw with his own eyes the results of those atrocities, when the few Spaniards, who escaped Castillo's clutches, came to seek asylum in England. There, at the great meeting, these men opened their shirts and showed the horrible scars of burned flesh. Angiolillo saw, and the effect surpassed a thousand theories; the impetus was beyond words, beyond arguments, beyond himself even.

Señor Antonio Canovas del Castillo, Prime Minister of Spain, sojourned at Santa Agueda. As usual in such cases, all strangers were kept away from his exalted presence. One exception was made, however, in the case of a distinguished looking, elegantly dressed Italian—the representative, it was understood, of an important journal. The distinguished gentleman was—Angiolillo.

Señor Canovas, about to leave his house, stepped on the veranda. Suddenly Angiolillo confronted him. A shot rang out, and Canovas was a corpse.

The wife of the Prime Minister rushed upon the scene. "Murderer! Murderer!" she cried, pointing at Angiolillo. The latter bowed. "Pardon, Madame," he said, "I respect you as a lady, but I regret that you were the wife of that man."

Calmly Angiolillo faced death. Death in its most terrible form—for the man whose soul was as a child's.

He was garroted. His body lay, sun-kissed, till the day hid in twilight. And the people came, and pointing the finger of terror and fear, they said: "There—the criminal—the cruel murderer."

How stupid, how cruel is ignorance! It misunderstands always, condemns always.

A remarkable parallel to the case of Angiolillo is to be found in the act of Gaetano Bresci, whose *Attentat* upon King Umberto made an American city famous.

Bresci came to this country, this land of opportunity, where one has but to try to meet with golden success. Yes, he too would try to succeed. He would work hard and faithfully. Work had no terrors for him, if it would only help him to independence, manhood, self-respect.

Thus full of hope and enthusiasm he settled in Paterson, New Jersey, and there found a lucrative job at six dollars per week in one of the weaving mills of the town. Six whole dollars per week was, no doubt, a fortune for Italy, but not enough to breathe on in the new country. He loved his little home. He was a good husband and devoted father to his *bambina* Bianca, whom he adored. He worked and worked for a number of years. He actually managed to save one hundred dollars out of his six dollars per week.

Bresci had an ideal. Foolish, I know, for a workingman to have an ideal,—the Anarchist paper published in Paterson, *La Questione Sociale.*

Every week, though tired from work, he would help to set up the paper. Until late hours he would assist, and when the little pioneer had exhausted all resources and his comrades were in despair, Bresci brought cheer and hope, one hundred dollars, the entire savings of years. That would keep the paper afloat.

In his native land people were starving. The crops had been poor, and the peasants saw themselves face to face with famine. They appealed to their good King Umberto; he would help. And he did. The wives of the peasants who had gone to the palace of the King, held up in mute silence their emaciated infants. Surely that would move him. And then the soldiers fired and killed those poor fools.

Bresci, at work in the weaving mill at Paterson, read of the horrible massacre. His mental eye beheld the defenseless women and innocent infants of his native land, slaughtered right before the good King. His soul recoiled in horror. At night he heard the groans of the wounded. Some may have been his comrades, his own flesh. Why, why these foul murders?

The little meeting of the Italian Anarchist group in Paterson ended almost in a fight. Bresci had demanded his hundred dollars. His comrades begged, implored him to give them a respite. The paper would go down if they were to return him his loan. But Bresci insisted on its return.

How cruel and stupid is ignorance. Bresci got the money, but lost the good will, the confidence of his comrades. They would have nothing more to do with one whose greed was greater than his ideals.

On the twenty-ninth of July, 1900, King Umberto was shot at Monzo. The young Italian weaver of Paterson, Gaetano Bresci, had taken the life of the good King.

Paterson was placed under police surveillance, everyone known as an Anarchist hounded and persecuted, and the act of Bresci ascribed to the teachings of Anarchism. As if the teachings of Anarchism in its extremist form could equal the force of those slain women and infants, who had pilgrimed to the King for aid. As if any spoken word, ever so eloquent, could burn into a human soul with such white heat as the lifeblood trickling drop by drop from those dying forms. The ordinary man is rarely moved either by word or deed; and those whose social kinship is the greatest living force need no appeal to respond—even as does steel to the magnet—to the wrongs and horrors of society.

If a social theory is a strong factor inducing acts of political violence, how are we to account for the recent violent outbreaks in India, where Anarchism has hardly been born. More than any other old philosophy, Hindu teachings have exalted passive resistance, the drifting of life, the Nirvana, as the highest spiritual ideal. Yet the social unrest in India is daily growing, and has only recently resulted in an act of political violence, the killing of Sir Curzon Wyllie by the Hindu Madan Lal Dhingra.[25]

If such a phenomenon can occur in a country socially and individually permeated for centuries with the spirit of passivity, can one question the tremendous, revolutionizing effect on human character exerted by great social iniquities? Can one doubt the logic, the justice of these words:

"Repression, tyranny, and indiscriminate punishment of innocent men have been the watchwords of the government of the alien domination in India ever since we began the commercial boycott of English goods. The tiger qualities of the British are much in evidence now in India. They think that by the strength of the sword they will keep down India! It is this arrogance that has brought about the bomb, and the more they tyrannize over a helpless and unarmed people, the more terrorism will grow. We may deprecate terrorism as outlandish and foreign to our culture, but it is inevitable as long as this tyranny continues, for it is not the terrorists that are to be blamed, but the tyrants who are responsible for it. It is the only resource for a helpless and unarmed people when brought to the verge of despair. It is never criminal on their part. The crime lies with the tyrant."[26]

Even conservative scientists are beginning to realize that heredity is not the sole factor moulding human character. Climate, food, occupation; nay, color, light, and sound must be considered in the study of human psychology.

If that be true, how much more correct is the contention that great social abuses will and must influence different minds and temperaments in a different way. And how utterly fallacious the stereotyped notion that the teachings of Anarchism, or certain exponents of these teachings, are responsible for the acts of political violence.

Anarchism, more than any other social theory, values human life above things. All Anarchists agree with Tolstoy in this fundamental truth: if the production of any commodity necessitates the sacrifice of human life, society should do without that commodity, but it cannot do without that life. That, however, nowise indicates

---

25   Madan Lal Dhingra (1883–1909), Indian revolutionary and pro-independence activist. While studying in London, he assassinated Sir William Hutt Curzon Wyllie, an official of the British Indian government.
26   *The Free Hindustan.*

THE PSYCHOLOGY OF POLITICAL VIOLENCE

that Anarchism teaches submission. How can it, when it knows that all suffering, all misery, all ills, result from the evil of submission?

Has not some American ancestor said, many years ago, that resistance to tyranny is obedience to God? And he was not an Anarchist even. I would say that resistance to tyranny is man's highest ideal. So long as tyranny exists, in whatever form, man's deepest aspiration must resist it as inevitably as man must breathe.

Compared with the wholesale violence of capital and government, political acts of violence are but a drop in the ocean. That so few resist is the strongest proof how terrible must be the conflict between their souls and unbearable social iniquities.

High strung, like a violin string, they weep and moan for life, so relentless, so cruel, so terribly inhuman. In a desperate moment the string breaks. Untuned ears hear nothing but discord. But those who feel the agonized cry understand its harmony; they hear in it the fulfillment of the most compelling moment of human nature.

Such is the psychology of political violence.

THE INDIVIDUAL, SOCIETY, AND THE STATE

T HE MINDS OF men are in confusion, for the very foundations of our civilization seem to be tottering. People are losing faith in the existing institutions, and the more intelligent realize that capitalist industrialism is defeating the very purpose it is supposed to serve.

The world is at a loss for a way out. Parliamentarism and democracy are on the decline. Salvation is being sought in Fascism and other forms of "strong" government.

The struggle of opposing ideas now going on in the world involves social problems urgently demanding a solution. The welfare of the individual and the fate of human society depend on the right answer to those questions. The crises of unemployment, war, disarmament, international relations, etc., are among those problems.

The State, government with its functions and powers, is now the subject of vital interest to every thinking man. Political developments in all civilized countries have brought the questions home. Shall we have a strong government? Are democracy and parliamentary government to be preferred, or is Fascism of one kind or another, dictatorship—monarchical, bourgeois or proletarian—the solution of the ills and difficulties that beset society today?

In other words, shall we cure the evils of democracy by more democracy, or shall we cut the Gordian knot of popular government with the sword of dictatorship?

My answer is neither the one nor the other. I am against dictatorship and Fascism as I am opposed to parliamentary regimes and so-called political democracy.

Nazism has been justly called an attack on civilization. This characterization applies with equal force to every form of dictatorship; indeed, to every kind of suppression and coercive authority. For what is civilization in the true sense? All progress has been essentially an enlargement of the liberties of the individual with a corresponding decrease of the authority wielded over him by external forces. This holds good in the realm of physical as well as of political and economic existence. In the physical world man has progressed to the extent in which he has subdued the forces of nature and made them useful to himself. Primitive man made a step on the road to progress when he first produced fire and thus triumphed over darkness, when he chained the wind or harnessed water.

What role did authority or government play in human endeavor for betterment, in invention and discovery? None whatever, or at least none that was helpful. It has always been the individual that has accomplished every miracle in that sphere, usually in spite of the prohibition, persecution and interference by authority, human and divine.

Similarly, in the political sphere, the road of progress lay in getting away more and more from the authority of the tribal chief or of the clan, of prince and king, of government, of the State. Economically, progress has meant greater well-being of ever larger numbers. Culturally, it has signified the result of all the other achievements—greater independence, political, mental and psychic.

Regarded from this angle, the problem of man's relation to the State assumes an entirely different significance. It is no more a question of whether dictatorship is preferable to democracy, or Italian Fascism superior to Hitlerism. A larger and far more vital question poses itself: Is political government, is the State, beneficial to mankind, and how does it affect the individual in the social scheme of things?

The individual is the true reality in life. A cosmos in himself, he does not exist for the State, nor for that abstraction called "society," or the "nation," which is only a collection of individuals. Man, the individual, has always been and necessarily is the sole source and motive power of evolution and progress. Civilization has been a continuous struggle of the individual or of groups of individuals against the State and even against "society," that is, against the majority subdued and hypnotized by the State and State worship. Man's greatest battles have been waged against man-made obstacles and artificial handicaps imposed upon him to paralyse his growth and development. Human thought has always been falsified by tradition and custom, and perverted false education in the interests of those who held power and enjoyed privileges. In other words, by the State and the ruling classes. This constant incessant conflict has been the history of mankind.

Individuality may be described as the consciousness of the individual as to what he is and how he lives. It is inherent in every human being and is a thing of growth. The State and social institutions come and go, but individuality remains and persists. The very essence of individuality is expression; the sense of dignity and independence is the soil wherein it thrives. Individuality is not the impersonal and mechanistic thing that the State treats as an "individual." The individual is not merely the result of heredity and environment, of cause and effect. He is that and a great deal more, a great deal else. The living man cannot be defined; he is the fountain-head of all life and all values; he is not a part of this or of that; he is a whole, an individual whole, a growing, changing, yet always constant whole.

Individuality is not to be confused with the various ideas and concepts of Individualism; much less with that "rugged individualism" which is only a masked attempt to repress and defeat the individual and his individuality. So-called Individualism is the social and economic *laissez-faire*: the exploitation of the masses by the classes by means of legal trickery, spiritual debasement and systematic indoctrination of the servile spirit, which process is known as "education." That corrupt and perverse "individualism" is the strait-jacket of individuality. It has converted life into a degrading race for externals, for possession, for social prestige and supremacy. Its highest wisdom is "the devil take the hindmost."

This "rugged individualism" has inevitably resulted in the greatest modern slavery, the crassest class distinctions, driving millions to the breadline. "Rugged individualism" has meant all the "individualism" for the masters, while the people are regimented into a slave caste to serve a handful of self-seeking "supermen." America is perhaps the best representative of this kind of individualism, in whose name political tyranny and social oppression are defended and held up as virtues; while every aspiration and attempt of man to gain freedom and social opportunity to live is denounced as "un-American" and evil in the name of that same individualism.

There was a time when the State was unknown. In his natural condition man existed without any State or organized government. People lived as families in small communities; they tilled the soil and practiced the arts and crafts. The individual, and later the family, was the unit of social life where each was free and the equal of his neighbor. Human society then was not a State but an association; a voluntary association for mutual protection and benefit. The elders and more experienced members were the guides and advisers of the people. They helped to manage the affairs of the life, not to rule and dominate the individual.

Political government and the State were a much later development, growing out of the desire of the stronger to take advantage of the weaker, of the few against the many. The State, ecclesiastical and secular, served to give an appearance of legality and right to the wrong done by the few to the many. That appearance of right was necessary the easier to rule the people, because no government can exist without the consent of the people, consent open, tacit or assumed. Constitutionalism and democracy are the modern forms of that alleged consent; the consent being inoculated and indoctrinated by what is called "education," at home, in the church, and in every other phase of life.

That consent is the belief in authority, in the necessity for it. At its base is the doctrine that man is evil, vicious, and too incompetent to know what is good for him. On this all government and oppression is built. God and the State exist and are supported by this dogma.

Yet the State is nothing but a name. It is an abstraction. Like other similar conceptions—nation, race, humanity—it has no organic reality. To call the State an organism shows a diseased tendency to make a fetish of words.

The State is a term for the legislative and administrative machinery whereby certain business of the people is transacted, and badly so. There is nothing sacred, holy or mysterious about it. The State has no more conscience or moral mission than a commercial company for working a coal mine or running a railroad.

The State has no more existence than gods and devils have. They are equally the reflex and creation of man, for man, the individual, is the only reality. The State is but the shadow of man, the shadow of his opaqueness, of his ignorance and fear.

Life begins and ends with man, the individual. Without him there is no race, no humanity, no State. No, not even "society" is possible without man. It is the individual who lives, breathes and suffers. His development, his advance, has been a continuous struggle against the fetishes of his own creation and particularly so against the "State."

In former days religious authority fashioned political life in the image of the Church. The authority of the State, the "rights" of rulers came from on high; power, like faith, was divine. Philosophers have written thick volumes to prove the sanctity of the State; some have even clad it with infallibility and with god-like attributes. Some have talked themselves into the insane notion that the State is "superhuman," the supreme reality, "the absolute."

Enquiry was condemned as blasphemy. Servitude was the highest virtue. By such precepts and training certain things came to be regarded as self-evident, as sacred of their truth, but because of constant and persistent repetition.

All progress has been essentially an unmasking of "divinity" and "mystery," of alleged sacred, eternal "truth"; it has been a gradual elimination of the abstract and the substitution in its place of the real, the concrete. In short, of facts against fancy, of knowledge against ignorance, of light against darkness.

That slow and arduous liberation of the individual was not accomplished by the aid of the State. On the contrary, it was by continuous conflict, by a life-and-death struggle with the State, that even the smallest vestige of independence and freedom has been won. It has cost mankind much time and blood to secure what little it has gained so far from kings, czars and governments.

The great heroic figure of that long Golgotha has been Man. It has always been the individual, often alone and singly, at other times in unity and co-operation with others of his kind, who has fought and bled in the age-long battle against suppression and oppression, against the powers that enslave and degrade him.

More than that and more significant: It was man, the individual, whose soul first rebelled against injustice and degradation; it was the individual who first conceived the idea of resistance to the conditions under which he chafed. In short, it is always the individual who is the parent of the liberating thought as well as of the deed.

This refers not only to political struggles, but to the entire gamut of human life and effort, in all ages and climes. It has always been the individual, the man of strong mind and will to liberty, who paved the way for every human advance, for every step toward a freer and better world; in science, philosophy and art, as well as in industry, whose genius rose to the heights, conceiving the "impossible," visualizing its realization and imbuing others with his enthusiasm to work and strive for it. Socially speaking, it was always the prophet, the seer, the idealist, who dreamed of a world more to his heart's desire and who served as the beacon light on the road to greater achievement.

The State, every government whatever its form, character or color—be it absolute or constitutional, monarchy or republic, Fascist, Nazi or Bolshevik—is by its very nature conservative, static, intolerant of change and opposed to it. Whatever changes it undergoes are always the result of pressure exerted upon it, pressure strong enough to compel the ruling powers to submit peaceably or otherwise, generally "otherwise"—that is, by revolution. Moreover, the inherent conservatism of government, of authority of any kind, unavoidably becomes reactionary. For two reasons: first, because it is in the nature of government not only to retain the power it has, but also to strengthen, widen and perpetuate it, nationally as well as internationally. The stronger authority grows, the greater the State and its power, the less it can tolerate a similar authority or political power alongside of itself. The psychology of government demands that its influence and prestige constantly grow, at home and abroad, and it exploits every opportunity to increase it. This tendency is motivated by the financial and commercial interests back of the government, represented and served by it. The fundamental *raison d'être* of every government to which, incidentally, historians of former days willfully shut their eyes, has become too obvious now even for professors to ignore.

The other factor which impels governments to become even more conservative and reactionary is their inherent distrust of the individual and fear of individuality. Our political and social scheme cannot afford to tolerate the individual and his constant quest for innovation. In "self-defense" the State therefore suppresses, persecutes, punishes and even deprives the individual of life. It is aided in this by every institution that stands for the preservation of the existing order. It resorts to every form of violence and force, and its efforts are supported by the "moral indignation" of the majority against the heretic, the social dissenter and the political rebel—the majority for centuries drilled in State worship, trained in discipline and obedience and subdued by the awe of authority in the home, the school, the church and the press.

The strongest bulwark of authority is uniformity; the least divergence from it is the greatest crime. The wholesale mechanization of modern life has increased uniformity a thousandfold. It is everywhere present, in habits, tastes, dress, thoughts and ideas. Its most concentrated dullness is "public opinion." Few have the courage to stand out against it. He who refuses to submit is at once labelled "queer," "different," and decried as a disturbing element in the comfortable stagnancy of modern life.

Perhaps even more than constituted authority, it is social uniformity and sameness that harass the individual most. His very "uniqueness," "separateness" and "differentiation" make him an alien, not only in his native place, but even in his own home.

Often more so than the foreign born who generally falls in with the established.

In the true sense one's native land, with its background of tradition, early impressions, reminiscences and other things dear to one, is not enough to make sensitive human beings feel at home. A certain atmosphere of "belonging," the consciousness of being "at one" with the people and environment, is more essential to one's feeling of home. This holds good in relation to one's family, the smaller local circle, as well as the larger phase of the life and activities commonly called one's country. The individual whose vision encompasses the whole world often feels nowhere so hedged in and out of touch with his surroundings than in his native land.

In pre-war times the individual could at least escape national and family boredom. The whole world was open to his longings and his quests. Now the world has become a prison, and life continual solitary confinement. Especially is this true since the advent of dictatorship, right and left.

Friedrich Nietzsche called the State a cold monster.[27] What would he have called the hideous beast in the garb of modern dictatorship? Not that government had ever allowed much scope to the individual; but the champions of the new State ideology do not grant even that much. "The individual is nothing," they declare, "it is the collectivity which counts." Nothing less than the complete surrender of the individual will satisfy the insatiable appetite of the new deity.

Strangely enough, the loudest advocates of this new gospel are to be found among the British and American intelligentsia. Just now they are enamored with the "dictatorship of the proletariat." In theory only, to be sure. In practice, they still prefer the few liberties in their own respective countries. They go to Russia for a short visit or as salesmen of the "revolution," but they feel safer and more comfortable at home.

Perhaps it is not only lack of courage which keeps these good Britishers and Americans in their native lands rather than in the millennium to come. Subconsciously there may lurk the feeling that individuality remains the most fundamental fact of all human association, suppressed and persecuted yet never defeated, and in the long run the victor.

The "genius of man," which is but another name for personality and individuality, bores its way through all the caverns of dogma, through the thick walls of tradition and custom, defying all taboos, setting authority at naught, facing contumely and the scaffold—ultimately to be blessed as prophet and martyr by succeeding generations. But for the "genius of man," that inherent, persistent quality of individuality, we would be still roaming the primeval forests.

Peter Kropotkin has shown what wonderful results this unique force of man's individuality has achieved when strengthened by co-operation with other

---

27   Friedrich Nietzsche (1844–1900), German philosopher best known for his critique of Western morality and philosophy.

individualities.[28] The one-sided and entirely inadequate Darwinian theory of the struggle for existence received its biological and sociological completion from the great Anarchist scientist and thinker. In his profound work, *Mutual Aid*, Kropotkin shows that in the animal kingdom, as well as in human society, co-operation—as opposed to internecine strife and struggle—has worked for the survival and evolution of the species. He demonstrated that only mutual aid and voluntary co-operation—not the omnipotent, all-devastating State—can create the basis for a free individual and associational life.

At present the individual is the pawn of the zealots of dictatorship and the equally obsessed zealots of "rugged individualism." The excuse of the former is its claim of a new objective. The latter does not even make a pretense of anything new. As a matter of fact "rugged individualism" has learned nothing and forgotten nothing. Under its guidance the brute struggle for physical existence is still kept up. Strange as it may seem, and utterly absurd as it is, the struggle for physical survival goes merrily on though the necessity for it has entirely disappeared. Indeed, the struggle is being continued apparently because there is no necessity for it. Does not so-called overproduction prove it? Is not the world-wide economic crisis an eloquent demonstration that the struggle for existence is being maintained by the blindness of "rugged individualism" at the risk of its own destruction?

One of the insane characteristics of this struggle is the complete negation of the relation of the producer to the things he produces. The average worker has no inner point of contact with the industry he is employed in, and he is a stranger to the process of production of which he is a mechanical part. Like any other cog of the machine, he is replaceable at any time by other similar depersonalized human beings.

The intellectual proletarian, though he foolishly thinks himself a free agent, is not much better off. He, too, has as little choice or self-direction, in his particular métier, as his brother who works with his hands. Material considerations and desire for greater social prestige are usually the deciding factors in the vocation of the intellectual. Added to these is the tendency to follow in the footsteps of family tradition, and become doctors, lawyers, teachers, engineers, etc. The groove requires less effort and personality. In consequence nearly everybody is out of place in our present scheme of things. The masses plod on, partly because their senses have been dulled by the deadly routine of work and because they must eke out an existence. This applies with even greater force to the political fabric of today. There is no place in its texture for free choice of independent thought and activity. There is a place only for voting and tax-paying puppets.

The interests of the State and those of the individual differ fundamentally and are antagonistic. The State and the political and economic institutions it supports

---

28   Pyotr Alexeyevich Kropotkin (1842–1921), Russian anarchist, historian, and philosopher who advocated anarcho-communism.

can exist only by fashioning the individual to their particular purpose; training him to respect "law and order"; teaching him obedience, submission and unquestioning faith in the wisdom and justice of government; above all, loyal service and complete self-sacrifice when the State commands it, as in war. The State puts itself and its interests even above the claims of religion and of God. It punishes religious or conscientious scruples against individuality because there is no individuality without liberty, and liberty is the greatest menace to authority.

The struggle of the individual against these tremendous odds is the more difficult—too often dangerous to life and limb—because it is not truth or falsehood which serves as the criterion of the opposition he meets. It is not the validity or usefulness of his thought or activity which rouses against him the forces of the State and of "public opinion." The persecution of the innovator and protestant has always been inspired by fear on the part of constituted authority of having its infallibility questioned and its power undermined.

Man's true liberation, individual and collective, lies in his emancipation from authority and from the belief in it. All human evolution has been a struggle in that direction and for that object. It is not invention and mechanics which constitute development. The ability to travel at the rate of 100 miles an hour is no evidence of being civilized. True civilization is to be measured by the individual, the unit of all social life; by his individuality and the extent to which it is free to have its being, to grow and expand unhindered by invasive and coercive authority.

Socially speaking, the criterion of civilization and culture is the degree of liberty and economic opportunity which the individual enjoys; of social and international unity and cooperation unrestricted by man-made laws and other artificial obstacles; by the absence of privileged castes and by the reality of liberty and human dignity; in short, by the true emancipation of the individual.

Political absolutism has been abolished because men have realized in the course of time that absolute power is evil and destructive. But the same thing is true of all power, whether it be the power of privilege, of money, of the priest, of the politician or of so-called democracy. In its effect on individuality it matters little what the particular character of coercion is—whether it be as black as Fascism, as yellow as Nazism or as pretentiously red as Bolshevism. It is power that corrupts and degrades both master and slave and it makes no difference whether the power is wielded by an autocrat, by parliament or Soviets. More pernicious than the power of a dictator is that of a class; the most terrible—the tyranny of a majority.

The long process of history has taught man that division and strife mean death, and that unity and co-operation advance his cause, multiply his strength and further his welfare. The spirit of government has always worked against the social application of this vital lesson, except where it served the State and aided its own particular interests. It is this anti-progressive and anti-social spirit of the State and of the privileged castes back of it which has been responsible for the bitter struggle between man and man. The individual and ever larger groups of individuals are beginning to see beneath the surface of the established order of things. No longer are they so blinded as in the past by the glare and tinsel of the State idea, and of the "blessings" of "rugged individualism." Man is reaching out for the wider scope of human relations which liberty alone can give. For true liberty is not a mere scrap of paper called "constitution," "legal right" or "law." It is not an abstraction derived from the non-reality known as "the State." It is not the negative thing of being free from something, because with such freedom you may starve to death. Real freedom, true liberty is positive: it is freedom to something; it is the liberty to be, to do; in short, the liberty of actual and active opportunity.

That sort of liberty is not a gift: it is the natural right of man, of every human being. It cannot be given; it cannot be conferred by any law or government. The need of it, the longing for it, is inherent in the individual. Disobedience to every form of coercion is the instinctive expression of it. Rebellion and revolution are the more or less conscious attempt to achieve it. Those manifestations, individual and social, are fundamentally expressions of the values of man. That those values may be nurtured, the community must realize that its greatest and most lasting asset is the unit—the individual.

In religion, as in politics, people speak of abstractions and believe they are dealing with realities. But when it does come to the real and the concrete, most people seem to lose vital touch with it. It may well be because reality alone is too matter-of-fact, too cold to enthuse the human soul. It can be aroused to enthusiasm only by things out of the commonplace, out of the ordinary. In other words, the Ideal is the spark that fires the imagination and hearts of men. Some ideal is needed to rouse man out of the inertia and humdrum of his existence and turn the abject slave into an heroic figure.

Right here, of course, comes the Marxist objector who has outmarxed Marx himself. To such a one, man is a mere puppet in the hands of that metaphysical Almighty called economic determinism or, more vulgarly, the class struggle. Man's will, individual and collective, his psychic life and mental orientation count for almost nothing with our Marxist and do not affect his conception of human history.

No intelligent student will deny the importance of the economic factor in the social growth and development of mankind. But only narrow and wilful dogmatism can persist in remaining blind to the important role played by an idea as conceived by the imagination and aspirations of the individual.

It were vain and unprofitable to attempt to balance one factor as against another in human experience. No one single factor in the complex of individual or social behavior can be designated as the factor of decisive quality. We know too little, and may never know enough, of human psychology to weigh and measure the relative values of this or that factor in determining man's conduct. To form such dogmas in their social connotation is nothing short of bigotry; yet, perhaps, it has its uses, for the very attempt to do so proved the persistence of the human will and confutes the Marxists.

Fortunately even some Marxists are beginning to see that all is not well with the Marxian creed. After all, Marx was but human—all too human—hence by no means infallible. The practical application of economic determinism in Russia is helping to clear the minds of the more intelligent Marxists. This can be seen in the trans-valuation of Marxian values going on in Socialist and even Communist ranks in some European countries. They are slowly realizing that their theory has overlooked the human element, *den Menschen* [the human being], as a Socialist paper put it. Important as the economic factor is, it is not enough. The rejuvenation of mankind needs the inspiration and energizing force of an ideal.

Such an ideal I see in Anarchism. To be sure, not in the popular misrepresenta-tions of Anarchism spread by the worshippers of the State and authority. I mean the philosophy of a new social order based on the released energies of the individual and the free association of liberated individuals.

Of all social theories Anarchism alone steadfastly proclaims that society exists for man, not man for society. The sole legitimate purpose of society is to serve the needs and advance the aspiration of the individual. Only by doing so can it justify its existence and be an aid to progress and culture.

The political parties and men savagely scrambling for power will scorn me as hopelessly out of tune with our time. I cheerfully admit the charge. I find comfort in the assurance that their hysteria lacks enduring quality. Their hosanna is but of the hour.

Man's yearning for liberation from all authority and power will never be soothed by their cracked song. Man's quest for freedom from every shackle is eternal. It must and will go on.

FEMINISM

THE TRAFFIC IN WOMEN

O UR REFORMERS HAVE suddenly made a great discovery—the white slave traffic. The papers are full of these "unheard-of conditions," and lawmakers are already planning a new set of laws to check the horror.

It is significant that whenever the public mind is to be diverted from a great social wrong, a crusade is inaugurated against indecency, gambling, saloons, etc. And what is the result of such crusades? Gambling is increasing, saloons are doing a lively business through back entrances, prostitution is at its height, and the system of pimps and cadets is but aggravated.

How is it that an institution, known almost to every child, should have been discovered so suddenly? How is it that this evil, known to all sociologists, should now be made such an important issue?

To assume that the recent investigation of the white slave traffic (and, by the way, a very superficial investigation) has discovered anything new, is, to say the least, very foolish. Prostitution has been, and is, a widespread evil, yet mankind goes on its business, perfectly indifferent to the sufferings and distress of the victims of prostitution. As indifferent, indeed, as mankind has remained to our industrial system, or to economic prostitution.

Only when human sorrows are turned into a toy with glaring colors will baby people become interested—for a while at least. The people are a very fickle baby that must have new toys every day. The "righteous" cry against the white slave traffic is such a toy. It serves to amuse the people for a little while, and it will help to create a few more fat political jobs—parasites who stalk about the world as inspectors, investigators, detectives, and so forth.

What is really the cause of the trade in women? Not merely white women, but yellow and black women as well. Exploitation, of course; the merciless Moloch of capitalism that fattens on underpaid labor, thus driving thousands of women and girls into prostitution. With Mrs. Warren[29] these girls feel, "Why waste your life working for a few shillings a week in a scullery, eighteen hours a day?"

Naturally our reformers say nothing about this cause. They know it well enough, but it doesn't pay to say anything about it. It is much more profitable to play the

---

29   Mrs. Warren is the protagonist of George Bernard Shaw's 1892 play (first performed in 1902), *Mrs. Warren's Profession*, about a former prostitute turned brothel proprietor.

Pharisee, to pretend an outraged morality, than to go to the bottom of things.

However, there is one commendable exception among the young writers: Reginald Wright Kauffman, whose work *The House of Bondage* is the first earnest attempt to treat the social evil—not from a sentimental Philistine viewpoint.[30] A journalist of wide experience, Mr. Kauffman proves that our industrial system leaves most women no alternative except prostitution. The women portrayed in *The House of Bondage* belong to the working class. Had the author portrayed the life of women in other spheres, he would have been confronted with the same state of affairs.

Nowhere is woman treated according to the merit of her work, but rather as a sex. It is therefore almost inevitable that she should pay for her right to exist, to keep a position in whatever line, with sex favors. Thus it is merely a question of degree whether she sells herself to one man, in or out of marriage, or to many men. Whether our reformers admit it or not, the economic and social inferiority of woman is responsible for prostitution.

Just at present our good people are shocked by the disclosures that in New York City alone one out of every ten women works in a factory, that the average wage received by women is six dollars per week for forty-eight to sixty hours of work, and that the majority of female wage workers face many months of idleness which leaves the average wage about $280 a year. In view of these economic horrors, is it to be wondered at that prostitution and the white slave trade have become such dominant factors?

Lest the preceding figures be considered an exaggeration, it is well to examine what some authorities on prostitution have to say:

"A prolific cause of female depravity can be found in the several tables, showing the description of the employment pursued, and the wages received, by the women previous to their fall, and it will be a question for the political economist to decide how far mere business consideration should be an apology on the part of employers for a reduction in their rates of remuneration, and whether the savings of a small percentage on wages is not more than counterbalanced by the enormous amount of taxation enforced on the public at large to defray the expenses incurred on account of a system of vice, *which is the direct result, in many cases, of insufficient compensation of honest labor.*"[31]

Our present-day reformers would do well to look into Dr. Sanger's book. There they will find that out of 2,000 cases under his observation, but few came from the middle classes, from well-ordered conditions, or pleasant homes. By far the largest majority were working girls and working women; some driven into prostitution through sheer want, others because of a cruel, wretched life at home, others again

---

30   Reginald Wright Kauffman (1877–1959), U.S. American author, editor, and journalist.
31   William Sanger, *The History of Prostitution: Its Extent, Causes, and Effects Throughout the World* (1858).

because of thwarted and crippled physical natures (of which I shall speak later on). Also it will do the maintainers of purity and morality good to learn that out of two thousand cases, 490 were married women, women who lived with their husbands. Evidently there was not much of a guaranty for their "safety and purity" in the sanctity of marriage.

Dr. Alfred Blaschko, in *Prostitution in the Nineteenth Century*, is even more emphatic in characterizing economic conditions as one of the most vital factors of prostitution.

"Although prostitution has existed in all ages, it was left to the nineteenth century to develop it into a gigantic social institution. The development of industry with vast masses of people in the competitive market, the growth and congestion of large cities, the insecurity and uncertainty of employment, has given prostitution an impetus never dreamed of at any period in human history."

And again Havelock Ellis, while not so absolute in dealing with the economic cause, is nevertheless compelled to admit that it is indirectly and directly the main cause.[32] Thus he finds that a large percentage of prostitutes is recruited from the servant class, although the latter have less care and greater security. On the other hand, Mr. Ellis does not deny that the daily routine, the drudgery, the monotony of the servant girl's lot, and especially the fact that she may never partake of the companionship and joy of a home, is no mean factor in forcing her to seek recreation and forgetfulness in the gaiety and glimmer of prostitution. In other words, the servant girl, being treated as a drudge, never having the right to herself, and worn out by the caprices of her mistress, can find an outlet, like the factory or shopgirl, only in prostitution.

The most amusing side of the question now before the public is the indignation of our "good, respectable people," especially the various Christian gentlemen, who are always to be found in the front ranks of every crusade. Is it that they are absolutely ignorant of the history of religion, and especially of the Christian religion? Or is it that they hope to blind the present generation to the part played in the past by the Church in relation to prostitution? Whatever their reason, they should be the last to cry out against the unfortunate victims of today, since it is known to every intelligent student that prostitution is of religious origin, maintained and fostered for many centuries, not as a shame, but as a virtue, hailed as such by the Gods themselves.

"It would seem that the origin of prostitution is to be found primarily in a religious custom, religion, the great conserver of social tradition, preserving in a transformed shape a primitive freedom that was passing out of the general social life. The typical example is that recorded by Herodotus, in the fifth century before Christ, at the Temple of Mylitta, the Babylonian Venus, where every woman, once in her life, had to come and give herself to the first stranger, who threw a coin in her lap, to

---

32   Havelock Ellis (1859–1939), British physicist and writer who studied human sexuality.

worship the goddess. Very similar customs existed in other parts of western Asia, in North Africa, in Cyprus, and other islands of the eastern Mediterranean, and also in Greece, where the temple of Aphrodite on the fort at Corinth possessed over a thousand hierodules, dedicated to the service of the goddess.

"The theory that religious prostitution developed, as a general rule, out of the belief that the generative activity of human beings possessed a mysterious and sacred influence in promoting the fertility of Nature, is maintained by all authoritative writers on the subject. Gradually, however, and when prostitution became an organized institution under priestly influence, religious prostitution developed utilitarian sides, thus helping to increase public revenue.

"The rise of Christianity to political power produced little change in policy. The leading fathers of the Church tolerated prostitution. Brothels under municipal protection are found in the thirteenth century. They constituted a sort of public service, the directors of them being considered almost as public servants."[33]

To this must be added the following from Dr. Sanger's work:

"Pope Clement II issued a bull that prostitutes would be tolerated if they pay a certain amount of their earnings to the Church.

"Pope Sixtus IV was more practical; from one single brothel, which he himself had built, he received an income of 20,000 ducats."

In modern times the Church is a little more careful in that direction. At least she does not openly demand tribute from prostitutes. She finds it much more profitable to go in for real estate, like Trinity Church, for instance, to rent out death traps at an exorbitant price to those who live off and by prostitution.

Much as I should like to, my space will not admit speaking of prostitution in Egypt, Greece, Rome, and during the Middle Ages. The conditions in the latter period are particularly interesting, inasmuch as prostitution was organized into guilds, presided over by a brothel queen. These guilds employed strikes as a medium of improving their condition and keeping a standard price. Certainly that is more practical a method than the one used by the modern wage-slave in society.

It would be one-sided and extremely superficial to maintain that the economic factor is the only cause of prostitution. There are others no less important and vital. That, too, our reformers know, but dare discuss even less than the institution that saps the very life out of both men and women. I refer to the sex question, the very mention of which causes most people moral spasms.

It is a conceded fact that woman is being reared as a sex commodity, and yet she is kept in absolute ignorance of the meaning and importance of sex. Everything dealing with that subject is suppressed, and persons who attempt to bring light into this terrible darkness are persecuted and thrown into prison. Yet it is nevertheless true that so long as a girl is not to know how to take care of herself, not to know

33   Havelock Ellis, *Studies in the Psychology of Sex, Vol. 6: Sex in Relation to Society* (1910).

the function of the most important part of her life, we need not be surprised if she becomes an easy prey to prostitution, or to any other form of a relationship which degrades her to the position of an object for mere sex gratification.

It is due to this ignorance that the entire life and nature of the girl is thwarted and crippled. We have long ago taken it as a self-evident fact that the boy may follow the call of the wild; that is to say, that the boy may, as soon as his sex nature asserts itself, satisfy that nature; but our moralists are scandalized at the very thought that the nature of a girl should assert itself. To the moralist prostitution does not consist so much in the fact that the woman sells her body, but rather that she sells it out of wedlock. That this is no mere statement is proved by the fact that marriage for monetary considerations is perfectly legitimate, sanctified by law and public opinion, while any other union is condemned and repudiated. Yet a prostitute, if properly defined, means nothing else than "any person for whom sexual relationships are subordinated to gain."[34]

"Those women are prostitutes who sell their bodies for the exercise of the sexual act and make of this a profession."[35]

In fact, Bonger goes further; he maintains that the act of prostitution is "intrinsically equal to that of a man or woman who contracts a marriage for economic reasons."

Of course, marriage is the goal of every girl, but as thousands of girls cannot marry, our stupid social customs condemn them either to a life of celibacy or prostitution. Human nature asserts itself regardless of all laws, nor is there any plausible reason why nature should adapt itself to a perverted conception of morality.

Society considers the sex experiences of a man as attributes of his general development, while similar experiences in the life of a woman are looked upon as a terrible calamity, a loss of honor and of all that is good and noble in a human being. This double standard of morality has played no little part in the creation and perpetuation of prostitution. It involves the keeping of the young in absolute ignorance on sex matters, which alleged "innocence," together with an overwrought and stifled sex nature, helps to bring about a state of affairs that our Puritans are so anxious to avoid or prevent.

Not that the gratification of sex must needs lead to prostitution; it is the cruel, heartless, criminal persecution of those who dare divert from the beaten track, which is responsible for it.

Girls, mere children, work in crowded, overheated rooms ten to twelve hours daily at a machine, which tends to keep them in a constant, over-excited sex state. Many of these girls have no home or comforts of any kind; therefore the street or some place of cheap amusement is the only means of forgetting their daily routine.

---

34   Yves Guyot, *La prostitution* (1882).
35   Willem Adriaan Bonger, *Criminalité et conditions économiques* (1905).

This naturally brings them into close proximity with the other sex. It is hard to say which of the two factors brings the girl's over-sexed condition to a climax, but it is certainly the most natural thing that a climax should result. That is the first step toward prostitution. Nor is the girl to be held responsible for it. On the contrary, it is altogether the fault of society, the fault of our lack of understanding, of our lack of appreciation of life in the making; especially is it the criminal fault of our moralists, who condemn a girl for all eternity, because she has gone from the "path of virtue"; that is, because her first sex experience has taken place without the sanction of the Church.

The girl feels herself a complete outcast, with the doors of home and society closed in her face. Her entire training and tradition is such that the girl herself feels depraved and fallen, and therefore has no ground to stand upon, or any hold that will lift her up, instead of dragging her down. Thus society creates the victims that it afterwards vainly attempts to get rid of. The meanest, most depraved and decrepit man still considers himself too good to take as his wife the woman whose grace he was quite willing to buy, even though he might thereby save her from a life of horror. Nor can she turn to her own sister for help. In her stupidity the latter deems herself too pure and chaste, not realizing that her own position is in many respects even more deplorable than her sister's of the street.

"The wife who married for money, compared with the prostitute," says Havelock Ellis, "is the true scab. She is paid less, gives much more in return in labor and care, and is absolutely bound to her master. The prostitute never signs away the right over her own person, she retains her freedom and personal rights, nor is she always compelled to submit to man's embrace."

Nor does the better-than-thou woman realize the apologist claim of Lecky that "though she may be the supreme type of vice, she is also the most efficient guardian of virtue. But for her, happy homes would be polluted, unnatural and harmful practice would abound."

Moralists are ever ready to sacrifice one-half of the human race for the sake of some miserable institution which they cannot outgrow. As a matter of fact, prostitution is no more a safeguard for the purity of the home than rigid laws are; a safeguard against prostitution. Fully fifty percent of married men are patrons of brothels. It is through this virtuous element that the married women—nay, even the children—are infected with venereal diseases. Yet society has not a word of condemnation for the man, while no law is too monstrous to be set in motion against the helpless victim. She is not only preyed upon by those who use her, but she is also absolutely at the mercy of every policeman and miserable detective on the beat, the officials at the station house, the authorities in every prison.

In a recent book by a woman who was for twelve years the mistress of a "house," are to be found the following figures: "The authorities compelled me to pay every month fines between $14.70 to $29.70, the girls would pay from $5.70 to $9.70 to the police." Considering that the writer did her business in a small city, that the amounts she gives do not include extra bribes and fines, one can readily see the tremendous revenue the police department derives from the blood money of its victims, whom it will not even protect. Woe to those who refuse to pay their toll; they would be rounded up like cattle, "if only to make a favorable impression upon the good cit-izens of the city, or if the powers needed extra money on the side. For the warped mind who believes that a fallen woman is incapable of human emotion it would be impossible to realize the grief, the disgrace, the tears, the wounded pride that was ours every time we were pulled in."

Strange, isn't it, that a woman who has kept a "house" should be able to feel that way? But stranger still that a good Christian world should bleed and fleece such women, and give them nothing in return except obloquy and persecution. Oh, for the charity of a Christian world!

Much stress is laid on white slaves being imported into America. How would America ever retain her virtue if Europe did not help her out? I will not deny that this may be the case in some instances, any more than I will deny that there are emis-saries of Germany and other countries luring economic slaves into America; but I absolutely deny that prostitution is recruited to any appreciable extent from Europe. It may be true that the majority of prostitutes of New York City are foreigners, but that is because the majority of the population is foreign. The moment we go to any other American city, to Chicago or the Middle West, we shall find that the number of foreign prostitutes is by far a minority.

Equally exaggerated is the belief that the majority of street girls in this city were engaged in this business before they came to America. Most of the girls speak excel-lent English, are Americanized in habits and appearance—a thing absolutely impos-sible unless they had lived in this country many years. That is, they were driven into prostitution by American conditions, by the thoroughly American custom for excessive display of finery and clothes, which, of course, necessitates money—money that cannot be earned in shops or factories.

In other words, there is no reason to believe that any set of men would go to the risk and expense of getting foreign products, when American conditions are over-flooding the market with thousands of girls. On the other hand, there is sufficient evidence to prove that the export of American girls for the purpose of prostitution is by no means a small factor.

Thus Clifford G. Roe, ex-Assistant State Attorney of Cook County, Ill., makes the open charge that New England girls are shipped to Panama for the express use of men in the employ of Uncle Sam. Mr. Roe adds that "there seems to be an under-ground railroad between Boston and Washington which many girls travel." Is it not significant that the railroad should lead to the very seat of Federal authority? That

Mr. Roe said more than was desired in certain quarters is proved by the fact that he lost his position. It is not practical for men in office to tell tales from school.

The excuse given for the conditions in Panama is that there are no brothels in the Canal Zone. That is the usual avenue of escape for a hypocritical world that dares not face the truth. Not in the Canal Zone, not in the city limits,—therefore prostitution does not exist.

Next to Mr. Roe, there is James Bronson Reynolds, who has made a thorough study of the white slave traffic in Asia. As a staunch American citizen and friend of the future Napoleon of America, Theodore Roosevelt, he is surely the last to discredit the virtue of his country. Yet we are informed by him that in Hong Kong, Shanghai, and Yokohama, the Augean stables of American vice are located. There American prostitutes have made themselves so conspicuous that in the Orient "American girl" is synonymous with prostitute. Mr. Reynolds reminds his countrymen that while Americans in China are under the protection of our consular representatives, the Chinese in America have no protection at all. Everyone who knows the brutal and barbarous persecution Chinese and Japanese endure on the Pacific Coast, will agree with Mr. Reynolds.

In view of the above facts it is rather absurd to point to Europe as the swamp whence come all the social diseases of America. Just as absurd is it to proclaim the myth that the Jews furnish the largest contingent of willing prey. I am sure that no one will accuse me of nationalistic tendencies. I am glad to say that I have developed out of them, as out of many other prejudices. If, therefore, I resent the statement that Jewish prostitutes are imported, it is not because of any Judaistic sympathies, but because of the facts inherent in the lives of these people. No one but the most superficial will claim that Jewish girls migrate to strange lands, unless they have some tie or relation that brings them there. The Jewish girl is not adventurous. Until recent years she had never left home, not even so far as the next village or town, except it were to visit some relative. Is it then credible that Jewish girls would leave their parents or families, travel thousands of miles to strange lands, through the influence and promises of strange forces? Go to any of the large incoming steamers and see for yourself if these girls do not come either with their parents, brothers, aunts, or other kinsfolk. There may be exceptions, of course, but to state that large numbers of Jewish girls are imported for prostitution, or any other purpose, is simply not to know Jewish psychology.

Those who sit in a glass house do wrong to throw stones about them; besides, the American glass house is rather thin, it will break easily, and the interior is anything but a gainly sight.

To ascribe the increase of prostitution to alleged importation, to the growth of the cadet system, or similar causes, is highly superficial. I have already referred to the former. As to the cadet system, abhorrent as it is, we must not ignore the fact that it is essentially a phase of modern prostitution,—a phase accentuated by suppression and graft, resulting from sporadic crusades against the social evil.

The procurer is no doubt a poor specimen of the human family, but in what manner is he more despicable than the policeman who takes the last cent from the street walker, and then locks her up in the station house? Why is the cadet more criminal, or a greater menace to society, than the owners of department stores and factories, who grow fat on the sweat of their victims, only to drive them to the streets? I make no plea for the cadet, but I fail to see why he should be mercilessly hounded, while the real perpetrators of all social iniquity enjoy immunity and respect. Then, too, it is well to remember that it is not the cadet who makes the prostitute. It is our sham and hypocrisy that create both the prostitute and the cadet.

Until 1894 very little was known in America of the procurer. Then we were attacked by an epidemic of virtue. Vice was to be abolished, the country purified at all cost. The social cancer was therefore driven out of sight, but deeper into the body. Keepers of brothels, as well as their unfortunate victims, were turned over to the tender mercies of the police. The inevitable consequence of exorbitant bribes, and the penitentiary, followed.

While comparatively protected in the brothels, where they represented a certain monetary value, the girls now found themselves on the street, absolutely at the mercy of the graft-greedy police. Desperate, needing protection and longing for affection, these girls naturally proved an easy prey for cadets, themselves the result of the spirit of our commercial age. Thus the cadet system was the direct outgrowth of police persecution, graft, and attempted suppression of prostitution. It were sheer folly to confound this modern phase of the social evil with the causes of the latter.

Mere suppression and barbaric enactments can serve but to embitter, and further degrade, the unfortunate victims of ignorance and stupidity. The latter has reached its highest expression in the proposed law to make humane treatment of prostitutes a crime, punishing any one sheltering a prostitute with five years' imprisonment and $10,000 fine. Such an attitude merely exposes the terrible lack of understanding of the true causes of prostitution, as a social factor, as well as manifesting the Puritanic spirit of the Scarlet Letter days.

There is not a single modern writer on the subject who does not refer to the utter futility of legislative methods in coping with the issue. Thus Dr. Blaschko finds that governmental suppression and moral crusades accomplish nothing save driving the evil into secret channels, multiplying its dangers to society. Havelock Ellis, the most thorough and humane student of prostitution, proves by a wealth of data that the more stringent the methods of persecution the worse the condition becomes. Among other data we learn that in France, "in 1560, Charles IX abolished brothels through an edict, but the numbers of prostitutes were only increased, while many new brothels appeared in unsuspected shapes, and were more dangerous. In spite of all such legislation, *or because of it,* there has been no country in which prostitution has played a more conspicuous part."[36]

An educated public opinion, freed from the legal and moral hounding of the prostitute, can alone help to ameliorate present conditions. Wilful shutting of eyes and ignoring of the evil as a social factor of modern life, can but aggravate matters. We must rise above our foolish notions of "better than thou," and learn to recognize in the prostitute a product of social conditions. Such a realization will sweep away the attitude of hypocrisy, and insure a greater understanding and more humane treatment. As to a thorough eradication of prostitution, nothing can accomplish that save a complete transvaluation of all accepted values—especially the moral ones—coupled with the abolition of industrial slavery.

---

36   Havelock Ellis, *Studies in the Psychology of Sex, Vol. 6: Sex in Relation to Society* (1910).

MARRIAGE AND LOVE

T HE POPULAR NOTION about marriage and love is that they are synonymous, that they spring from the same motives, and cover the same human needs. Like most popular notions this also rests not on actual facts, but on superstition.

Marriage and love have nothing in common; they are as far apart as the poles; are, in fact, antagonistic to each other. No doubt some marriages have been the result of love. Not, however, because love could assert itself only in marriage; much rather is it because few people can completely outgrow a convention. There are today large numbers of men and women to whom marriage is naught but a farce, but who submit to it for the sake of public opinion. At any rate, while it is true that some marriages are based on love, and while it is equally true that in some cases love continues in married life, I maintain that it does so regardless of marriage, and not because of it.

On the other hand, it is utterly false that love results from marriage. On rare occasions one does hear of a miraculous case of a married couple falling in love after marriage, but on close examination it will be found that it is a mere adjustment to the inevitable. Certainly the growing-used to each other is far away from the spontaneity, the intensity, and beauty of love, without which the intimacy of marriage must prove degrading to both the woman and the man.

Marriage is primarily an economic arrangement, an insurance pact. It differs from the ordinary life insurance agreement only in that it is more binding, more exacting. Its returns are insignificantly small compared with the investments. In taking out an insurance policy one pays for it in dollars and cents, always at liberty to discontinue payments. If, however, woman's premium is a husband, she pays for it with her name, her privacy, her self-respect, her very life, "until death doth part." Moreover, the marriage insurance condemns her to life-long dependency, to parasitism, to complete uselessness, individual as well as social. Man, too, pays his toll, but as his sphere is wider, marriage does not limit him as much as woman. He feels his chains more in an economic sense.

Thus Dante's motto over *Inferno* applies with equal force to marriage: "Ye who enter here leave all hope behind."

That marriage is a failure none but the very stupid will deny. One has but to glance over the statistics of divorce to realize how bitter a failure marriage really is. Nor will the stereotyped Philistine argument that the laxity of divorce laws and the growing looseness of woman account for the fact that: first, every twelfth marriages ends in divorce; second, that since 1870 divorces have increased from 28 to 73 for every hundred thousand population; third, that adultery, since 1867, as ground for divorce, has increased 270.8 percent; fourth, that desertion increased 369.8 percent.

Added to these startling figures is a vast amount of material, dramatic and literary, further elucidating this subject. Robert Herrick, in *Together;* Pinero, in *Mid-Channel;* Eugene Walter, in *Paid in Full,* and scores of other writers are discussing the barrenness, the monotony, the sordidness, the inadequacy of marriage as a factor for harmony and understanding.

The thoughtful social student will not content himself with the popular superficial excuse for this phenomenon. He will have to dig down deeper into the very life of the sexes to know why marriage proves so disastrous.

Edward Carpenter says that behind every marriage stands the life-long environment of the two sexes; an environment so different from each other that man and woman must remain strangers. Separated by an insurmountable wall of superstition, custom, and habit, marriage has not the potentiality of developing knowledge of, and respect for, each other, without which every union is doomed to failure.

Henrik Ibsen, the hater of all social shams, was probably the first to realize this great truth. Nora leaves her husband, not—as the stupid critic would have it—because she is tired of her responsibilities or feels the need of woman's rights, but because she has come to know that for eight years she had lived with a stranger and borne him children. Can there be anything more humiliating, more degrading than a life-long proximity between two strangers? No need for the woman to know anything of the man, save his income. As to the knowledge of the woman—what is there to know except that she has a pleasing appearance? We have not yet outgrown the theologic myth that woman has no soul, that she is a mere appendix to man, made out of his rib just for the convenience of the gentleman who was so strong that he was afraid of his own shadow.

Perchance the poor quality of the material whence woman comes is responsible for her inferiority. At any rate, woman has no soul—what is there to know about her? Besides, the less soul a woman has the greater her asset as a wife, the more readily will she absorb herself in her husband. It is this slavish acquiescence to man's superiority that has kept the marriage institution seemingly intact for so long a period. Now that woman is coming into her own, now that she is actually growing aware of herself as a being outside of the master's grace, the sacred institution of marriage is gradually being undermined, and no amount of sentimental lamentation can stay it.

From infancy, almost, the average girl is told that marriage is her ultimate goal; therefore her training and education must be directed towards that end. Like the mute beast fattened for slaughter, she is prepared for that. Yet, strange to say, she is allowed to know much less about her function as wife and mother than the ordinary artisan of his trade. It is indecent and filthy for a respectable girl to know anything of the marital relation. Oh, for the inconsistency of respectability, that needs the marriage vow to turn something which is filthy into the purest and most sacred arrangement that none dare question or criticize. Yet that is exactly the attitude of the average upholder of marriage. The prospective wife and mother is kept in complete ignorance of her only asset in the competitive field—sex. Thus she enters into life-long relations with a man only to find herself shocked, repelled, outraged beyond measure by the most natural and healthy instinct, sex. It is safe to say that a large percentage of the unhappiness, misery, distress, and physical suffering of matrimony is due to the criminal ignorance in sex matters that is being extolled as a great virtue. Nor is it at all an exaggeration when I say that more than one home has been broken up because of this deplorable fact.

If, however, woman is free and big enough to learn the mystery of sex without the sanction of State or Church, she will stand condemned as utterly unfit to become the wife of a "good" man, his goodness consisting of an empty head and plenty of money. Can there be anything more outrageous than the idea that a healthy, grown woman, full of life and passion, must deny nature's demand, must subdue her most intense craving, undermine her health and break her spirit, must stunt her vision, abstain from the depth and glory of sex experience until a "good" man comes along to take her unto himself as a wife? That is precisely what marriage means. How can such an arrangement end except in failure? This is one, though not the least important, factor of marriage, which differentiates it from love.

Ours is a practical age. The time when Romeo and Juliet risked the wrath of their fathers for love, when Gretchen exposed herself to the gossip of her neighbors for love, is no more. If, on rare occasions, young people allow themselves the luxury of romance, they are taken in care, by the elders, drilled and pounded until they become "sensible."

The moral lesson instilled in the girl is not whether the man has aroused her love, but rather is it, "How much?" The important and only God of practical American life: Can the man make a living? Can he support a wife? That is the only thing that justifies marriage. Gradually this saturates every thought of the girl; her dreams are not of moonlight and kisses, of laughter and tears; she dreams of shopping tours and bargain counters. This soul-poverty and sordidness are the elements inherent in the marriage institution. The State and the Church approve of no other ideal, simply because it is the one that necessitates the State and Church control of men and women.

Doubtless there are people who continue to consider love above dollars and cents. Particularly is this true of that class whom economic necessity has forced to become self-supporting. The tremendous change in woman's position, wrought by that mighty factor, is indeed phenomenal when we reflect that it is but a short time since she has entered the industrial arena. Six million women wage-earners; six million women, who have the equal right with men to be exploited, to be robbed, to go on strike; aye, to starve even. Anything more, my lord? Yes, six million wage-workers in every walk of life, from the highest brain work to the most difficult menial labor in the mines and on the railroad tracks; yes, even detectives and policemen. Surely the emancipation is complete.

Yet with all that, but a very small number of the vast army of women wage-workers look upon work as a permanent issue, in the same light as does man. No matter how decrepit the latter, he has been taught to be independent, self-supporting. Oh, I know that no one is really independent in our economic treadmill; still, the poorest specimen of a man hates to be a parasite; to be known as such, at any rate.

The woman considers her position as worker transitory, to be thrown aside for the first bidder. That is why it is infinitely harder to organize women than men. "Why should I join a union? I am going to get married, to have a home." Has she not been taught from infancy to look upon that as her ultimate calling? She learns soon enough that the home, though not so large a prison as the factory, has more solid doors and bars. It has a keeper so faithful that naught can escape him. The most tragic part, however, is that the home no longer frees her from wage-slavery; it only increases her task.

According to the latest statistics submitted before a Committee "on labor and wages, and congestion of population," ten percent of the wage workers in New York City alone are married, yet they must continue to work at the most poorly paid labor in the world. Add to this horrible aspect the drudgery of housework, and what remains of the protection and glory of the home? As a matter of fact, even the middle-class girl in marriage cannot speak of her home, since it is the man who creates her sphere. It is not important whether the husband is a brute or a darling. What I wish to prove is that marriage guarantees woman a home only by the grace of her husband. There she moves about in *his* home, year after year, until her aspect of life and human affairs becomes as flat, narrow, and drab as her surroundings. Small wonder if she becomes a nag, petty, quarrelsome, gossipy, unbearable, thus driving the man from the house. She could not go, if she wanted to; there is no place to go. Besides, a short period of married life, of complete surrender of all faculties, absolutely incapacitates the average woman for the outside world. She becomes reckless in appearance, clumsy in her movements, dependent in her decisions, cowardly in her judgment, a weight and a bore, which most men grow to hate and despise. Wonderfully inspiring atmosphere for the bearing of life, is it not?

But the child, how is it to be protected, if not for marriage? After all, is not that the most important consideration? The sham, the hypocrisy of it! Marriage protecting the child, yet thousands of children destitute and homeless. Marriage protecting the child, yet orphan asylums and reformatories overcrowded, the Society for the

Prevention of Cruelty to Children keeping busy in rescuing the little victims from "loving" parents, to place them under more loving care, the Gerry Society. Oh, the mockery of it!

Marriage may have the power to "bring the horse to water," but has it ever made him drink? The law will place the father under arrest, and put him in convict's clothes; but has that ever stilled the hunger of the child? If the parent has no work, or if he hides his identity, what does marriage do then? It invokes the law to bring the man to "justice," to put him safely behind closed doors; his labor, however, goes not to the child, but to the State. The child receives but a blighted memory of its father's stripes.

As to the protection of the woman,—therein lies the curse of marriage. Not that it really protects her, but the very idea is so revolting, such an outrage and insult on life, so degrading to human dignity, as to forever condemn this parasitic institution.

It is like that other paternal arrangement—capitalism. It robs man of his birth-right, stunts his growth, poisons his body, keeps him in ignorance, in poverty and dependence, and then institutes charities that thrive on the last vestige of man's self-respect.

The institution of marriage makes a parasite of woman, an absolute dependent. It incapacitates her for life's struggle, annihilates her social consciousness, paralyzes her imagination, and then imposes its gracious protection, which is in reality a snare, a travesty on human character.

If motherhood is the highest fulfillment of woman's nature, what other protection does it need save love and freedom? Marriage but defiles, outrages, and corrupts her fulfillment. Does it not say to woman, Only when you follow me shall you bring forth life? Does it not condemn her to the block, does it not degrade and shame her if she refuses to buy her right to motherhood by selling herself? Does not marriage only sanction motherhood, even though conceived in hatred, in compulsion? Yet, if motherhood be of free choice, of love, of ecstasy, of defiant passion, does it not place a crown of thorns upon an innocent head and carve in letters of blood the hideous epithet, Bastard? Were marriage to contain all the virtues claimed for it, its crimes against motherhood would exclude it forever from the realm of love.

Love, the strongest and deepest element in all life, the harbinger of hope, of joy, of ecstasy; love, the defier of all laws, of all conventions; love, the freest, the most powerful moulder of human destiny; how can such an all-compelling force be syn-onymous with that poor little State and Church-begotten weed, marriage?

Free love? As if love is anything but free! Man has bought brains, but all the mil-lions in the world have failed to buy love. Man has subdued bodies, but all the power on earth has been unable to subdue love. Man has conquered whole nations, but all his armies could not conquer love. Man has chained and fettered the spirit, but he has been utterly helpless before love. High on a throne, with all the splendor and pomp his gold can command, man is yet poor and desolate, if love passes him by.

And if it stays, the poorest hovel is radiant with warmth, with life and color. Thus love has the magic power to make of a beggar a king. Yes, love is free; it can dwell in no other atmosphere. In freedom it gives itself unreservedly, abundantly, completely. All the laws on the statutes; all the courts in the universe, cannot tear it from the soil, once love has taken root. If, however, the soil is sterile, how can marriage make it bear fruit? It is like the last desperate struggle of fleeting life against death.

Love needs no protection; it is its own protection. So long as love begets life no child is deserted, or hungry, or famished for the want of affection. I know this to be true. I know women who became mothers in freedom by the men they loved. Few children in wedlock enjoy the care, the protection, the devotion free motherhood is capable of bestowing.

The defenders of authority dread the advent of a free motherhood, lest it will rob them of their prey. Who would fight wars? Who would create wealth? Who would make the policeman, the jailer, if woman were to refuse the indiscriminate breeding of children? The race, the race! shouts the king, the president, the capitalist, the priest. The race must be preserved, though woman be degraded to a mere machine,—and the marriage institution is our only safety valve against the pernicious sex-awakening of woman. But in vain these frantic efforts to maintain a state of bondage. In vain, too, the edicts of the Church, the mad attacks of rulers, in vain even the arm of the law. Woman no longer wants to be a party to the production of a race of sickly, feeble, decrepit, wretched human beings, who have neither the strength nor moral courage to throw off the yoke of poverty and slavery. Instead she desires fewer and better children, begotten and reared in love and through free choice; not by compulsion, as marriage imposes. Our pseudo-moralists have yet to learn the deep sense of responsibility toward the child, that love in freedom has awakened in the breast of woman. Rather would she forego forever the glory of motherhood than bring forth life in an atmosphere that breathes only destruction and death. And if she does become a mother, it is to give to the child the deepest and best her being can yield. To grow with the child is her motto; she knows that in that manner alone can she help build true manhood and womanhood.

Ibsen must have had a vision of a free mother, when, with a master stroke, he portrayed Mrs. Alving.[37] She was the ideal mother because she had outgrown marriage and all its horrors, because she had broken her chains, and set her spirit free to soar until it returned a personality, regenerated and strong. Alas, it was too late to rescue her life's joy, her Oswald; but not too late to realize that love in freedom is the only condition of a beautiful life. Those who, like Mrs. Alving, have paid with blood and tears for their spiritual awakening, repudiate marriage as an imposition, a shallow, empty mockery. They know, whether love last but one brief span of time or for

---

37   Mrs. Alving is the central character in Norwegian playwright Henrik Ibsen's 1891 play *Ghosts*. She is a widowed mother forced to make choices according to hollow moral codes.

eternity, it is the only creative, inspiring, elevating basis for a new race, a new world.

In our present pygmy state love is indeed a stranger to most people. Misunderstood and shunned, it rarely takes root; or if it does, it soon withers and dies. Its delicate fiber cannot endure the stress and strain of the daily grind. Its soul is too complex to adjust itself to the slimy woof of our social fabric. It weeps and moans and suffers with those who have need of it, yet lack the capacity to rise to love's summit.

Someday, someday men and women will rise, they will reach the mountain peak, they will meet big and strong and free, ready to receive, to partake, and to bask in the golden rays of love. What fancy, what imagination, what poetic genius can foresee even approximately the potentialities of such a force in the life of men and women. If the world is ever to give birth to true companionship and oneness, not marriage, but love will be the parent.

THE TRAGEDY OF WOMAN'S EMANCIPATION

I BEGIN WITH an admission: Regardless of all political and economic theories, treating of the fundamental differences between various groups within the human race, regardless of class and race distinctions, regardless of all artificial boundary lines between woman's rights and man's rights, I hold that there is a point where these differentiations may meet and grow into one perfect whole.

With this I do not mean to propose a peace treaty. The general social antagonism which has taken hold of our entire public life today, brought about through the force of opposing and contradictory interests, will crumble to pieces when the reorganization of our social life, based upon the principles of economic justice, shall have become a reality.

Peace or harmony between the sexes and individuals does not necessarily depend on a superficial equalization of human beings; nor does it call for the elimination of individual traits and peculiarities. The problem that confronts us today, and which the nearest future is to solve, is how to be one's self and yet in oneness with others, to feel deeply with all human beings and still retain one's own characteristic qualities. This seems to me to be the basis upon which the mass and the individual, the true democrat and the true individuality, man and woman, can meet without antagonism and opposition. The motto should not be: Forgive one another; rather, Understand one another. The oft-quoted sentence of Madame de Staël: "To understand everything means to forgive everything," has never particularly appealed to me; it has the odor of the confessional; to forgive one's fellow-being conveys the idea of pharisaical superiority. To understand one's fellow-being suffices. The admission partly represents the fundamental aspect of my views on the emancipation of woman and its effect upon the entire sex.

Emancipation should make it possible for woman to be human in the truest sense. Everything within her that craves assertion and activity should reach its fullest expression; all artificial barriers should be broken, and the road towards greater freedom cleared of every trace of centuries of submission and slavery.

This was the original aim of the movement for woman's emancipation. But the results so far achieved have isolated woman and have robbed her of the fountain springs of that happiness which is so essential to her. Merely external emancipation has made of the modern woman an artificial being, who reminds one of the products of French arboriculture with its arabesque trees and shrubs, pyramids, wheels, and wreaths; anything, except the forms which would be reached by the expression of her own inner qualities. Such artificially grown plants of the female sex are to be found in large numbers, especially in the so-called intellectual sphere of our life.

Liberty and equality for woman! What hopes and aspirations these words awakened when they were first uttered by some of the noblest and bravest souls of those days. The sun in all his light and glory was to rise upon a new world; in this world woman was to be free to direct her own destiny—an aim certainly worthy of the great enthusiasm, courage, perseverance, and ceaseless effort of the tremendous host of pioneer men and women, who staked everything against a world of prejudice and ignorance.

My hopes also move towards that goal, but I hold that the emancipation of woman, as interpreted and practically applied today, has failed to reach that great end. Now, woman is confronted with the necessity of emancipating herself from emancipation, if she really desires to be free. This may sound paradoxical, but is, nevertheless, only too true.

What has she achieved through her emancipation? Equal suffrage in a few States. Has that purified our political life, as many well-meaning advocates predicted? Certainly not. Incidentally, it is really time that persons with plain, sound judgment should cease to talk about corruption in politics in a boarding-school tone. Corruption of politics has nothing to do with the morals, or the laxity of morals, of various political personalities. Its cause is altogether a material one. Politics is the reflex of the business and industrial world, the mottos of which are: "To take is more blessed than to give"; "buy cheap and sell dear"; "one soiled hand washes the other." There is no hope even that woman, with her right to vote, will ever purify politics.

Emancipation has brought woman economic equality with man; that is, she can choose her own profession and trade; but as her past and present physical training has not equipped her with the necessary strength to compete with man, she is often compelled to exhaust all her energy, use up her vitality, and strain every nerve in order to reach the market value. Very few ever succeed, for it is a fact that women teachers, doctors, lawyers, architects, and engineers are neither met with the same confidence as their male colleagues, nor receive equal remuneration. And those that do reach that enticing equality, generally do so at the expense of their physical and psychical well-being. As to the great mass of working girls and women, how much independence is gained if the narrowness and lack of freedom of the home is exchanged for the narrowness and lack of freedom of the factory, sweat-shop, department store, or office? In addition is the burden which is laid on many women of looking after a "home, sweet home" —cold, dreary, disorderly, uninviting—after a day's hard work. Glorious independence! No wonder that hundreds of girls are so willing to accept the first offer of marriage, sick and tired of their "independence" behind the counter, at the sewing or typewriting machine. They are just as ready to marry as girls of the middle class, who long to throw off the yoke of parental supremacy. A so-called independence which leads only to earning the merest subsistence is not so enticing, not so ideal, that one could expect woman to sacrifice everything for it. Our highly praised independence is, after all, but a slow process of dulling and stifling woman's nature, her love instinct, and her mother instinct.

Nevertheless, the position of the working girl is far more natural and human than that of her seemingly more fortunate sister in the more cultured professional walks of life—teachers, physicians, lawyers, engineers, etc., who have to make a dignified, proper appearance, while the inner life is growing empty and dead.

The narrowness of the existing conception of woman's independence and emancipation; the dread of love for a man who is not her social equal; the fear that love will rob her of her freedom and independence; the horror that love or the joy of motherhood will only hinder her in the full exercise of her profession—all these together make of the emancipated modern woman a compulsory vestal, before whom life, with its great clarifying sorrows and its deep, entrancing joys, rolls on without touching or gripping her soul.

Emancipation, as understood by the majority of its adherents and exponents, is of too narrow a scope to permit the boundless love and ecstasy contained in the deep emotion of the true woman, sweetheart, mother, in freedom.

The tragedy of the self-supporting or economically free woman does not lie in too many, but in too few experiences. True, she surpasses her sister of past generations in knowledge of the world and human nature; it is just because of this that she feels deeply the lack of life's essence, which alone can enrich the human soul, and without which the majority of women have become mere professional automatons.

That such a state of affairs was bound to come was foreseen by those who realized that, in the domain of ethics, there still remained many decaying ruins of the time of the undisputed superiority of man; ruins that are still considered useful. And, what is more important, a goodly number of the emancipated are unable to get along without them. Every movement that aims at the destruction of existing institutions and the replacement thereof with something more advanced, more perfect, has followers who in theory stand for the most radical ideas, but who, nevertheless, in their everyday practice, are like the average Philistine, feigning respectability and clamoring for the good opinion of their opponents. There are, for example, Socialists, and even Anarchists, who stand for the idea that property is robbery, yet who will grow indignant if anyone owe them the value of a half-dozen pins.

The same Philistine can be found in the movement for woman's emancipation. Yellow journalists and milk-and-water litterateurs have painted pictures of the emancipated woman that make the hair of the good citizen and his dull companion stand up on end. Every member of the woman's rights movement was pictured as a George

Sand in her absolute disregard of morality. Nothing was sacred to her. She had no respect for the ideal relation between man and woman. In short, emancipation stood only for a reckless life of lust and sin; regardless of society, religion, and morality. The exponents of woman's rights were highly indignant at such misrepresentation, and, lacking humor, they exerted all their energy to prove that they were not at all as bad as they were painted, but the very reverse. Of course, as long as woman was the slave of man, she could not be good and pure, but now that she was free and independent she would prove how good she could be and that her influence would have a purifying effect on all institutions in society. True, the movement for woman's rights has broken many old fetters, but it has also forged new ones. The great movement of *true* emancipation has not met with a great race of women who could look liberty in the face. Their narrow, Puritanical vision banished man, as a disturber and doubtful character, out of their emotional life. Man was not to be tolerated at any price, except perhaps as the father of a child, since a child could not very well come to life without a father. Fortunately, the most rigid Puritans never will be strong enough to kill the innate craving for motherhood. But woman's freedom is closely allied with man's freedom, and many of my so-called emancipated sisters seem to overlook the fact that a child born in freedom needs the love and devotion of each human being about him, man as well as woman. Unfortunately, it is this narrow conception of human relations that has brought about a great tragedy in the lives of the modern man and woman.

About fifteen years ago appeared a work from the pen of the brilliant Norwegian Laura Marholm, called *Woman, a Character Study*.[38] She was one of the first to call attention to the emptiness and narrowness of the existing conception of woman's emancipation, and its tragic effect upon the inner life of woman. In her work Laura Marholm speaks of the fate of several gifted women of international fame: the genius Eleonora Duse; the great mathematician and writer Sonya Kovalevskaia; the artist and poet-nature Marie Bashkirtzeff, who died so young. Through each description of the lives of these women of such extraordinary mentality runs a marked trail of unsatisfied craving for a full, rounded, complete, and beautiful life, and the unrest and loneliness resulting from the lack of it. Through these masterly psychological sketches one cannot help but see that the higher the mental development of woman, the less possible it is for her to meet a congenial mate who will see in her, not only sex, but also the human being, the friend, the comrade and strong individuality, who cannot and ought not lose a single trait of her character.

The average man with his self-sufficiency, his ridiculously superior airs of patronage towards the female sex, is an impossibility for woman as depicted in the

---

38   Laura Marholm (1854–1928), Latvian writer born of a German mother and Danish father known for her novels, criticism, and biographies. In 1897 she published *Studies in the Psychology of Woman*, about real-life women in Scandinavia.

Character Study by Laura Marholm. Equally impossible for her is the man who can see in her nothing more than her mentality and her genius, and who fails to awaken her woman nature.

A rich intellect and a fine soul are usually considered necessary attributes of a deep and beautiful personality. In the case of the modern woman, these attributes serve as a hindrance to the complete assertion of her being. For over a hundred years the old form of marriage, based on the Bible, "till death doth part," has been denounced as an institution that stands for the sovereignty of the man over the woman, of her complete submission to his whims and commands, and absolute dependence on his name and support. Time and again it has been conclusively proved that the old matrimonial relation restricted woman to the function of man's servant and the bearer of his children. And yet we find many emancipated women who prefer marriage, with all its deficiencies, to the narrowness of an unmarried life narrow and unendurable because of the chains of moral and social prejudice that cramp and bind her nature.

The explanation of such inconsistency on the part of many advanced women is to be found in the fact that they never truly understood the meaning of emancipation. They thought that all that was needed was independence from external tyrannies; the internal tyrants, far more harmful to life and growth—ethical and social conventions—were left to take care of themselves; and they have taken care of themselves. They seem to get along as beautifully in the heads and hearts of the most active exponents of woman's emancipation, as in the heads and hearts of our grandmothers.

These internal tyrants, whether they be in the form of public opinion or what will mother say, or brother, father, aunt, or relative of any sort; what will Mrs. Grundy, Mr. Comstock,[39] the employer, the Board of Education say? All these busybodies, moral detectives, jailers of the human spirit, what will they say? Until woman has learned to defy them all, to stand firmly on her own ground and to insist upon her own unrestricted freedom, to listen to the voice of her nature, whether it call for life's greatest treasure, love for a man, or her most glorious privilege, the right to give birth to a child, she cannot call herself emancipated. How many emancipated women are brave enough to acknowledge that the voice of love is calling, wildly beating against their breasts demanding to be heard, to be satisfied.

The French writer Jean Reibrach, in one of his novels, *New Beauty*, attempts to picture the ideal, beautiful, emancipated woman. This ideal is embodied in a young girl, a physician. She talks very cleverly and wisely of how to feed infants; she is kind, and administers medicines free to poor mothers. She converses with a young man of her acquaintance about the sanitary conditions of the future, and how various bacilli and germs shall be exterminated by the use of stone walls and floors, and by

---

39   Anthony Comstock (1844–1915), anti-vice activist, United States Postal Inspector, and secretary of the New York Society for the Suppression of Vice. He is known as the creator of the Comstock "Chastity" Laws which targeted birth control.

the doing away with rugs and hangings. She is, of course, very plainly and practically dressed, mostly in black. The young man, who, at their first meeting, was overawed by the wisdom of his emancipated friend, gradually learns: to understand her, and recognizes one fine day that he loves her. They are young, and she is kind and beautiful, and though always in rigid attire, her appearance is softened by a spotlessly clean white collar and cuffs. One would expect that he would tell her of his love, but he is not one to commit romantic absurdities. Poetry and the enthusiasm of love cover their blushing faces before the pure beauty of the lady. He silences the voice of his nature, and remains correct. She, too, is always exact, always rational, always well behaved. I fear if they had formed a union, the young man would have risked freezing to death. I must confess that I can see nothing beautiful in this new beauty, who is as cold as the stone walls and floors she dreams of. Rather would I have the love songs of romantic ages, rather Don Juan and Madame Venus, rather an elopement by ladder and rope on a moonlight night, followed by the father's curse, mother's moans, and the moral comments of neighbors, than correctness and propriety measured by yardsticks. If love does not know how to give and take without restrictions, it is not love, but a transaction that never fails to lay stress on a plus and a minus.

The greatest shortcoming of the emancipation of the present day lies in its artificial stiffness and its narrow respectabilities, which produce an emptiness in woman's soul that will not let her drink from the fountain of life. I once remarked that there seemed to be a deeper relationship between the old-fashioned mother and hostess, ever on the alert for the happiness of her little ones and the comfort of those she loved, and the truly new woman, than between the latter and her average emancipated sister. The disciples of emancipation pure and simple declared me a heathen, fit only for the stake. Their blind zeal did not let them see that my comparison between the old and the new was merely to prove that a goodly number of our grandmothers had more blood in their veins, far more humor and wit, and certainly a greater amount of naturalness, kind-heartedness, and simplicity, than the majority of our emancipated professional women who fill the colleges, halls of learning, and various offices. This does not mean a wish to return to the past, nor does it condemn woman to her old sphere, the kitchen and the nursery.

Salvation lies in an energetic march onward towards a brighter and clearer future. We are in need of unhampered growth out of old traditions and habits. The movement for woman's emancipation has so far made but the first step in that direction. It is to be hoped that it will gather strength to make another. The right to vote, or equal civil rights, may be good demands, but true emancipation begins neither at the polls nor in courts. It begins in woman's soul. History tells us that every oppressed class gained true liberation from its masters through its own efforts. It is necessary that woman learn that lesson, that she realize that her freedom will reach as far as her power to achieve her freedom reaches. It is, therefore, far more important for her to begin with her inner regeneration, to cut loose from the weight of prejudices, traditions, and customs, The demand for equal rights in every vocation of life is just and fair; but, after all, the most vital right is the right to love and be loved. Indeed, if partial emancipation is to become a complete and true emancipation of woman, it will have to do away with the ridiculous notion that to be loved, to be sweetheart and mother, is synonymous with being slave or subordinate. It will have to do away with the absurd notion of the dualism of the sexes, or that man and woman represent two antagonistic worlds.

Pettiness separates; breadth unites. Let us be broad and big. Let us not overlook vital things because of the bulk of trifles confronting us. A true conception of the relation of the sexes will not admit of conqueror and conquered; it knows of but one great thing: to give of one's self boundlessly, in order to find one's self richer, deeper, better. That alone can fill the emptiness, and transform the tragedy of woman's emancipation into joy, limitless joy.

VICTIMS OF MORALITY

Not so very long ago I attended a meeting addressed by Anthony Comstock,[40] who has for forty years been the guardian of American morals. A more incoherent, ignorant ramble I have never heard from any platform.

The question that presented itself to me, listening to the commonplace, bigoted talk of the man, was, How could anyone so limited and unintelligent wield the power of censor and dictator over a supposedly democratic nation? True, Comstock has the law to back him. Forty years ago, when puritanism was even more rampant than today, completely shutting out the light of reason and progress, Comstock succeeded, through shady machination and political wire pulling, to introduce a bill which gave him complete control over the Post Office Department—a control which has proved disastrous to the freedom of the press, as well as the right of privacy of the American citizen.

Since then, Comstock has broken into the private chambers of people, has confiscated personal correspondence, as well as works of art, and has established a system of espionage and graft which would put Russia to shame. Yet the law does not explain the power of Anthony Comstock. There is something else, more terrible than the law. It is the narrow puritanic spirit, as represented in the sterile minds of the Young-Men-and-Old-Maid's Christian Union, Temperance Union, Sabbath Union, Purity League, etc. A spirit which is absolutely blind to the simplest manifestations of life; hence stands for stagnation and decay. As in antebellum days, these old fossils lament the terrible immorality of our time. Science, art, literature, the drama, are at the mercy of bigoted censorship and legal procedure, with the result that America, with all her boastful claims to progress and liberty is still steeped in the densest provincialism.

The smallest dominion in Europe can boast of an art free from the fetters of morality, an art that has the courage to portray the great social problems of our time. With the sharp edge of critical analysis, it cuts into every social ulcer, every wrong, demanding fundamental changes and the transvaluation of accepted values. Satire, wit, humor, as well as the most intensely serious modes of expression, are being employed to lay bare our conventional social and moral lies. In America we would seek in vain for such a medium, since even the attempt at it is made impossible by the

---

40   See note 39 above.

rigid régime, by the moral dictator and his clique.

The nearest approach, however, is our muckrakers, who have no doubt rendered great service along economic and social lines. Whether the muckrakers have or have not helped to change conditions, at least they have torn the mask from the lying face of our smug and self-satisfied society.

Unfortunately, the Lie of Morality still stalks about in fine feathers, since no one dares to come within hailing distance of that holy of holies. Yet it is safe to say that no other superstition is so detrimental to growth, so enervating and paralyzing to the minds and hearts of the people, as the superstition of Morality.

The most pathetic, and in a way discouraging, aspect of the situation is a certain element of liberals, and even of radicals, men and women apparently free from religious and social spooks. But before the monster of Morality they are as prostrate as the most pious of their kind—which is an additional proof to the extent to which the morality worm has eaten into the system of its victims and how far-going and thorough the measures must be which are to drive it out again.

Needless to say, society is obsessed by more than one morality. Indeed, every institution of today has its own moral standard. Nor could they ever have maintained themselves, were it not for religion, which acts as a shield, and for morality, which acts as the mask. This explains the interest of the exploiting rich in religion and morality. The rich preach, foster, and finance both, as an investment that pays good returns. Through the medium of religion they have paralyzed the mind of the people, just as morality has enslaved the spirit. In other words, religion and morality are a much better whip to keep people in submission than even the club and the gun.

To illustrate: The Property Morality declares that that institution is sacred. Woe to anyone that dares to question the sanctity of Property, or sins against it! Yet everyone knows that Property is robbery; that it represents the accumulated efforts of millions, who themselves are propertyless. And what is more terrible, the more poverty stricken the victim of Property Morality is, the greater his respect and awe for that master. Thus we hear advanced people, even so-called class-conscious workingmen, decry as immoral such methods as sabotage and direct action, because they aim at Property.

Verily, if the victims themselves are so blinded by the Property Morality, what need one expect from the masters? It therefore seems high time to bring home the fact that until the workers will lose respect for the instrument of their material enslavement, they need hope for no relief.

However, it is with the effect of Morality upon women that I am here mostly concerned. So disastrous, so paralyzing has this effect been, that some even of the most advanced among my sisters never thoroughly outgrow it.

It is Morality which condemns woman to the position of a celibate, a prostitute, or a reckless, incessant breeder of hapless children.

First, as to the celibate, the famished and withered human plant. When still a young, beautiful flower, she falls in love with a respectable young man. But Morality decrees that unless he can marry the girl, she must never know the raptures of love, the ecstasy of passion, which reaches its culminating expression in the sex embrace. The respectable young man is willing to marry, but the Property Morality, the Family and Social Moralities decree that he must first make his pile, must save up enough to establish a home and be able to provide for a family. The young people must wait, often many long, weary years.

Meanwhile the respectable young man, excited through the daily association and contact with his sweetheart, seeks an outlet for his nature in return for money. In ninety-nine cases out of a hundred, he will be infected, and when he is materially able to marry, he will infect his wife and possible offspring. And the young flower, with every fiber aglow with the fire of life, with all her being crying out for love and passion? She has no outlet. She develops headaches, insomnia, hysteria; grows embittered, quarrelsome, and soon becomes a faded, withered, joyless being, a nuisance to herself and everyone else. No wonder Stirner preferred the grisette to the maiden grown gray with virtue.

There is nothing more pathetic, nothing more terrible, than this gray-grown victim of a gray-grown Morality. This applies even with greater force to the masses of professional middle-class girls, than to those of the people. Through economic necessity the latter are thrust into life's jungle at an early age; they grow up with their male companions in the factory and shop, or at play and dance. The result is a more normal expression of their physical instincts. Then too, the young men and women of the people are not so hide-bound by externalities, and often follow the call of love and passion regardless of ceremony and tradition.

But the overwrought and oversexed middle-class girl, hedged in her narrow confines with family and social traditions, guarded by a thousand eyes, afraid of her own shadow—the yearning of her inmost being for the man or the child, must turn to cats, dogs, canary birds, or the Bible Class. Such is the cruel dictum of Morality, which is daily shutting out love, light, and joy from the lives of innumerable victims.

Now, as to the prostitute. In spite of laws, ordinances, persecution, and prisons; in spite of segregation, registration, vice crusades, and other similar devices, the prostitute is the real specter of our age. She sweeps across the plains like a fire burning into every nook of life, devastating, destroying.

After all, she is paying back, in a very small measure, the curse and horrors society has strewn in her path. She, weary with the tramp of ages, harassed and driven from pillar to post, at the mercy of all, is yet the Nemesis of modern times, the avenging angel, ruthlessly wielding the sword of fire. For has she not the man in her power? And, through him, the home, the child, the race. Thus she slays, and is herself the most brutally slain.

What has made her? Whence does she come? Morality, the Morality which is merciless in its attitude to women. Once she dared to be herself, to be true to her nature, to life, there is no return: the woman is thrust out from the pale and protection of society. The prostitute becomes the victim of Morality, even as the withered old maid is its victim. But the prostitute is victimized by still other forces, foremost among them the Property Morality, which compels woman to sell herself as a sex commodity for a dollar per, out of wedlock, or for fifteen dollars a week, in the sacred fold of matrimony. The latter is no doubt safer, more respected, more recognized, but of the two forms of prostitution the girl of the street is the least hypocritical, the least debased, since her trade lacks the pious mask of hypocrisy; and yet she is hounded, fleeced, outraged, and shunned, by the very powers that have made her: the financier, the priest, the moralist, the judge, the jailor, and the detective, not to forget her sheltered, respectably virtuous sister, who is the most relentless and brutal in her persecution of the prostitute.

Morality and its victim, the mother—what a terrible picture! Is there indeed anything more terrible, more criminal, than our glorified sacred function of motherhood? The woman, physically and mentally unfit to be a mother, yet condemned to breed; the woman, economically taxed to the very last spark of energy, yet forced to breed; the woman, tied to a man she loathes, whose very sight fills her with horror, yet made to breed; the woman, worn and used-up from the process of procreation, yet coerced to breed, more, ever more. What a hideous thing, this much-lauded motherhood! No wonder thousands of women risk mutilation, and prefer even death to this curse of the cruel imposition of the spook of Morality. Five thousand are yearly sacrificed upon the altar of this monster, that will not stand for prevention but would cure by abortion. Five thousand soldiers in the battle for their physical and spiritual freedom, and as many thousands more who are crippled and mutilated rather than bring forth life in a society based on decay and destruction.

Is it because the modern woman wants to shirk responsibility, or that she lacks love for her offspring, that she is driven to the most drastic and dangerous means to avoid bearing children? Only shallow, bigoted minds can bring such an accusation. Else they would know that the modern woman has become race-conscious, sensitive to the needs and rights of the child, as the unit of the race, and that therefore the modern woman has a sense of responsibility and humanity, which was quite foreign to her grandmother.

With the economic war raging all around her, with strife, misery, crime, disease, and insanity staring her in the face, with numberless little children ground into gold dust, how can the self- and race-conscious woman become a mother? Morality cannot answer this question. It can only dictate, coerce, or condemn—and how many women are strong enough to face this condemnation, to defy the moral dicta? Few, indeed. Hence they fill the factories, the reformatories, the homes for feeble minded, the prisons, the insane asylums, or they die in the attempt to prevent child-birth. Oh, Motherhood, what crimes are committed in thy name! What hosts are laid at your feet, Morality, destroyer of life!

Fortunately, the Dawn is emerging from the chaos and darkness. Woman is awakening, she is throwing off the nightmare of Morality; she will no longer be bound. In her love for the man, she is not concerned in the contents of his pocketbook, but in the wealth of his nature, which alone is the fountain of life and joy. Nor does she need the sanction of the State. Her love is sanction enough for her. Thus she can abandon herself to the man of her choice, as the flowers abandon themselves to dew and light, in freedom, beauty, and ecstasy.

Through her re-born consciousness as a unit, a personality, a race builder, she will become a mother only if she desires the child, and if she can give to the child, even before its birth, all that her nature and intellect can yield: harmony, health, comfort, beauty, and, above all, understanding, reverence, and love, which is the only fertile soil for new life, a new being.

Morality has no terrors for her who has risen beyond good and evil. And though Morality may continue to devour its victims, it is utterly powerless in the face of the modern spirit, that shines in all its glory upon the brow of man and woman, liberated and unafraid.

LIBERATION

PRISONS: A SOCIAL CRIME AND FAILURE

IN 1849 FYODOR Dostoyevsky wrote on the wall of his prison cell the following story of *The Priest and the Devil*:[41]

"'Hello, you little fat father!' the devil said to the priest. 'What made you lie so to those poor, misled people? What tortures of hell did you depict? Don't you know they are already suffering the tortures of hell in their earthly lives? Don't you know that you and the authorities of the State are my representatives on earth? It is you that make them suffer the pains of hell with which you threaten them. Don't you know this? Well, then, come with me!'

"The devil grabbed the priest by the collar, lifted him high in the air, and carried him to a factory, to an iron foundry. He saw the workmen there running and hurrying to and fro, and toiling in the scorching heat. Very soon the thick, heavy air and the heat are too much for the priest. With tears in his eyes, he pleads with the devil: 'Let me go! Let me leave this hell!'

"'Oh, my dear friend, I must show you many more places.' The devil gets hold of him again and drags him off to a farm. There he sees workmen threshing the grain. The dust and heat are insufferable. The overseer carries a knout, and unmercifully beats anyone who falls to the ground overcome by hard toil or hunger.

"Next the priest is taken to the huts where these same workers live with their families—dirty, cold, smoky, ill-smelling holes. The devil grins. He points out the poverty and hardships which are at home here.

"'Well, isn't this enough?' he asks. And it seems as if even he, the devil, pities the people. The pious servant of God can hardly bear it. With uplifted hands he begs: 'Let me go away from here. Yes, yes! This is hell on earth!'

"'Well, then, you see. And you still promise them another hell. You torment them, torture them to death mentally when they are already all but dead physically! Come on! I will show you one more hell—one more, the very worst.'

"He took him to a prison and showed him a dungeon, with its foul air and the many human forms, robbed of all health and energy, lying on the floor, covered with vermin that were devouring their poor, naked, emaciated bodies.

---

41   Fyodor Dostoevsky (1821–1881), Russian novelist who served four years of hard labor in Siberia followed by six years of compulsory military service after being found guilty of participating in a literary group that read books banned in Tsarist Russia.

"'Take off your silken clothes,' said the devil to the priest, 'put on your ankles heavy chains such as these unfortunates wear; lie down on the cold and filthy floor—and then talk to them about a hell that still awaits them!'

"'No, no!' answered the priest, 'I cannot think of anything more dreadful than this. I entreat you, let me go away from here!'

"'Yes, this is hell. There can be no worse hell than this. Did you not know it? Did you not know that these men and women whom you are frightening with the picture of a hell hereafter—did you not know that they are in hell right here, before they die?"

This was written fifty years ago in dark Russia, on the wall of one of the most horrible prisons. Yet who can deny that the same applies with equal force to the present time, even to American prisons?

With all our boasted reforms, our great social changes, and our far-reaching discoveries, human beings continue to be sent to the worst of hells, wherein they are outraged, degraded, and tortured, that society may be "protected" from the phantoms of its own making.

Prison, a social protection? What monstrous mind ever conceived such an idea? Just as well say that health can be promoted by a widespread contagion.

After eighteen months of horror in an English prison, Oscar Wilde gave to the world his great masterpiece, *The Ballad of Reading Gaol*:[42]

The vilest deeds, like poison weeds,
Bloom well in prison-air;
It is only what is good in Man
That wastes and withers there:
Pale Anguish keeps the heavy gate,
And the Warder is Despair.

Society goes on perpetuating this poisonous air, not realizing that out of it can come naught but the most poisonous results.

We are spending at the present $3,500,000 per day, $1,000,095,000 per year, to maintain prison institutions, and that in a democratic country,—a sum almost as large as the combined output of wheat, valued at $750,000,000, and the output of coal, valued at $350,000,000. Professor Bushnell of Washington, D. C., estimates the cost of prisons at $6,000,000,000 annually, and Dr. G. Frank Lydston, an eminent American writer on crime, gives $5,000,000,000 annually as a reasonable figure.[43] Such unheard-of expenditure for the purpose of maintaining vast armies of human

42   Oscar Wilde (1854–1900), Irish playwright, novelist, and critic who was sentenced to four years of hard labor for homosexuality. He published *The Ballad of Reading Gaol* in 1898 as an indictment of British moralism, a personal account of his love for Lord Alfred Douglas, and to advocate for prison reform.
43   For context, $1,000,000,000 is equivalent to $31,186,947,368 in 2022 U.S. dollars.

beings caged up like wild beasts![44]

Yet crimes are on the increase. Thus we learn that in America there are four and a half times as many crimes to every million population today as there were twenty years ago.

The most horrible aspect is that our national crime is murder, not robbery, embezzlement, or rape, as in the South. London is five times as large as Chicago, yet there are one hundred and eighteen murders annually in the latter city, while only twenty in London. Nor is Chicago the leading city in crime, since it is only seventh on the list, which is headed by four Southern cities, and San Francisco and Los Angeles. In view of such a terrible condition of affairs, it seems ridiculous to prate of the protection society derives from its prisons.

The average mind is slow in grasping a truth, but when the most thoroughly organized, centralized institution, maintained at an excessive national expense, has proven a complete social failure, the dullest must begin to question its right to exist. The time is past when we can be content with our social fabric merely because it is "ordained by divine right," or by the majesty of the law.

The widespread prison investigations, agitation, and education during the last few years are conclusive proof that men are learning to dig deep into the very bottom of society, down to the causes of the terrible discrepancy between social and individual life.

Why, then, are prisons a social crime and a failure? To answer this vital question it behooves us to seek the nature and cause of crimes, the methods employed in coping with them, and the effects these methods produce in ridding society of the curse and horror of crimes.

First, as to the *nature* of crime:

Havelock Ellis divides crime into four phases, the political, the passional, the insane, and the occasional. He says that the political criminal is the victim of an attempt of a more or less despotic government to preserve its own stability. He is not necessarily guilty of an unsocial offense; he simply tries to overturn a certain political order which may itself be anti-social. This truth is recognized all over the world, except in America where the foolish notion still prevails that in a Democracy there is no place for political criminals. Yet John Brown was a political criminal; so were the Chicago Anarchists; so is every striker. Consequently, says Havelock Ellis, the political criminal of our time or place may be the hero, martyr, saint of another age. Lombroso calls the political criminal the true precursor of the progressive movement of humanity.

"The criminal by passion is usually a man of wholesome birth and honest life, who under the stress of some great, unmerited wrong has wrought justice for himself."[45]

---

44   George Frank Lydston, *The Diseases of Society (The Vice and Crime Problem)* (1904).
45   Havelock Ellis, *The Criminal* (first published 1890).

Mr. Hugh C. Weir, in *The Menace of the Police,* cites the case of Jim Flaherty, a criminal by passion, who, instead of being saved by society, is turned into a drunkard and a recidivist, with a ruined and poverty-stricken family as the result.

A more pathetic type is Archie, the victim in Brand Whitlock's novel, *The Turn of the Balance,* the greatest American exposé of crime in the making. Archie, even more than Flaherty, was driven to crime and death by the cruel inhumanity of his surroundings, and by the unscrupulous hounding of the machinery of the law. Archie and Flaherty are but the types of many thousands, demonstrating how the legal aspects of crime, and the methods of dealing with it, help to create the disease which is undermining our entire social life.

"The insane criminal really can no more be considered a criminal than a child, since he is mentally in the same condition as an infant or an animal."[46]

The law already recognizes that, but only in rare cases of a very flagrant nature, or when the culprit's wealth permits the luxury of criminal insanity. It has become quite fashionable to be the victim of paranoia. But on the whole the "sovereignty of justice" still continues to punish criminally insane with the whole severity of its power. Thus Mr. Ellis quotes from Dr. Richter's statistics showing that in Germany one hundred and six madmen, out of one hundred and forty-four criminally insane, were condemned to severe punishment.

The occasional criminal "represents by far the largest class of our prison population, hence is the greatest menace to social well-being." What is the cause that compels a vast army of the human family to take to crime, to prefer the hideous life within prison walls to the life outside? Certainly that cause must be an iron master, who leaves its victims no avenue of escape, for the most depraved human being loves liberty.

This terrific force is conditioned in our cruel social and economic arrangement. I do not mean to deny the biologic, physiologic, or psychologic factors in creating crime; but there is hardly an advanced criminologist who will not concede that the social and economic influences are the most relentless, the most poisonous germs of crime. Granted even that there are innate criminal tendencies, it is none the less true that these tendencies find rich nutrition in our social environment.

There is close relation, says Havelock Ellis, between crimes against the person and the price of alcohol, between crimes against property and the price of wheat. He quotes Quetelet and Lacassagne, the former looking upon society as the preparer of crime, and the criminals as instruments that execute them. The latter finds that "the social environment is the cultivation medium of criminality; that the criminal is the microbe, an element which only becomes important when it finds the medium which causes it to ferment; *every society has the criminals it deserves.*"

The most "prosperous" industrial period makes it impossible for the worker to

---

46   Ibid.

earn enough to keep up health and vigor. And as prosperity is, at best, an imaginary condition, thousands of people are constantly added to the host of the unemployed. From East to West, from South to North, this vast army tramps in search of work or food, and all they find is the workhouse or the slums. Those who have a spark of self-respect left, prefer open defiance, prefer crime to the emaciated, degraded position of poverty.

Edward Carpenter estimates that five-sixths of indictable crimes consist in some violation of property rights; but that is too low a figure. A thorough investigation would prove that nine crimes out of ten could be traced, directly or indirectly, to our economic and social iniquities, to our system of remorseless exploitation and robbery. There is no criminal so stupid but recognizes this terrible fact, though he may not be able to account for it.

A collection of criminal philosophy, which Havelock Ellis, Lombroso, and other eminent men have compiled, shows that the criminal feels only too keenly that it is society that drives him to crime. A Milanese thief said to Lombroso: "I do not rob, I merely take from the rich their superfluities; besides, do not advocates and merchants rob?" A murderer wrote: "Knowing that three-fourths of the social virtues are cowardly vices, I thought an open assault on a rich man would be less ignoble than the cautious combination of fraud." Another wrote: "I am imprisoned for stealing a half dozen eggs. Ministers who rob millions are honored. Poor Italy!" An educated convict said to Mr. Davitt: "The laws of society are framed for the purpose of securing the wealth of the world to power and calculation, thereby depriving the larger portion of mankind of its rights and chances. Why should they punish me for taking by somewhat similar means from those who have taken more than they had a right to?" The same man added: "Religion robs the soul of its independence; patriotism is the stupid worship of the world for which the well-being and the peace of the inhabitants were sacrificed by those who profit by it, while the laws of the land, in restraining natural desires, were waging war on the manifest spirit of the law of our beings. Compared with this," he concluded, "thieving is an honorable pursuit."

Verily, there is greater truth in this philosophy than in all the law-and-moral books of society.

The economic, political, moral, and physical factors being the microbes of crime, how does society meet the situation?

The methods of coping with crime have no doubt undergone several changes, but mainly in a theoretic sense. In practice, society has retained the primitive motive in dealing with the offender; that is, revenge. It has also adopted the theologic idea; namely, punishment; while the legal and "civilized" methods consist of deterrence or terror, and reform. We shall presently see that all four modes have failed utterly, and that we are today no nearer a solution than in the dark ages.

The natural impulse of the primitive man to strike back, to avenge a wrong, is out of date. Instead, the civilized man, stripped of courage and daring, has delegated to an organized machinery the duty of avenging his wrongs, in the foolish belief that the State is justified in doing what he no longer has the manhood or consistency to do. The "majesty of the law" is a reasoning thing; it would not stoop to primitive instincts. Its mission is of a "higher" nature. True, it is still steeped in the theologic muddle, which proclaims punishment as a means of purification, or the vicarious atonement of sin. But legally and socially the statute exercises punishment, not merely as an infliction of pain upon the offender, but also for its terrifying effect upon others.

What is the real basis of punishment, however? The notion of a free will, the idea that man is at all times a free agent for good or evil; if he chooses the latter, he must be made to pay the price. Although this theory has long been exploded, and thrown upon the dustheap, it continues to be applied daily by the entire machinery of government, turning it into the most cruel and brutal tormentor of human life. The only reason for its continuance is the still more cruel notion that the greater the terror punishment spreads, the more certain its preventative effect.

Society is using the most drastic methods in dealing with the social offender. Why do they not deter? Although in America a man is supposed to be considered innocent until proven guilty, the instruments of law, the police, carry on a reign of terror, making indiscriminate arrests, beating, clubbing, bullying people, using the barbarous method of the "third degree," subjecting their unfortunate victims to the foul air of the station house, and the still fouler language of its guardians. Yet crimes are rapidly multiplying, and society is paying the price. On the other hand, it is an open secret that when the unfortunate citizen has been given the full "mercy" of the law, and for the sake of safety is hidden in the worst of hells, his real Calvary begins. Robbed of his rights as a human being, degraded to a mere automaton without will or feeling, dependent entirely upon the mercy of brutal keepers, he daily goes through a process of dehumanization, compared with which savage revenge was mere child's play.

There is not a single penal institution or reformatory in the United States where men are not tortured "to be made good," by means of the black-jack, the club, the strait-jacket, the water-cure, the "humming bird" (an electrical contrivance run along the human body), the solitary, the bull-ring, and starvation diet. In these institutions his will is broken, his soul degraded, his spirit subdued by the deadly monotony and routine of prison life. In Ohio, Illinois, Pennsylvania, Missouri, and in the South, these horrors have become so flagrant as to reach the outside world, while in most other prisons the same Christian methods still prevail. But prison walls rarely allow the agonized shrieks of the victims to escape—prison walls are thick, they dull the sound. Society might with greater immunity abolish all prisons at once, than to hope for protection from these twentieth-century chambers of horrors.

Year after year the gates of prison hells return to the world an emaciated, deformed, will-less, shipwrecked crew of humanity, with the Cain mark on their foreheads, their hopes crushed, all their natural inclinations thwarted. With nothing but hunger and inhumanity to greet them, these victims soon sink back into crime as the only possibility of existence. It is not at all an unusual thing to find men and women who have spent half their lives—nay, almost their entire existence—in prison. I know a woman on Blackwell's Island, who had been in and out thirty-eight times; and through a friend I learn that a young boy of seventeen, whom he had nursed and cared for in the Pittsburg penitentiary, had never known the meaning of liberty. From the reformatory to the penitentiary had been the path of this boy's life, until, broken in body, he died a victim of social revenge. These personal experiences are substantiated by extensive data giving overwhelming proof of the utter futility of prisons as a means of deterrence or reform.

Well-meaning persons are now working for a new departure in the prison question,—reclamation, to restore once more to the prisoner the possibility of becoming a human being. Commendable as this is, I fear it is impossible to hope for good results from pouring good wine into a musty bottle. Nothing short of a complete reconstruction of society will deliver mankind from the cancer of crime. Still, if the dull edge of our social conscience would be sharpened, the penal institutions might be given a new coat of varnish. But the first step to be taken is the renovation of the social consciousness, which is in a rather dilapidated condition. It is sadly in need to be awakened to the fact that crime is a question of degree, that we all have the rudiments of crime in us, more or less, according to our mental, physical, and social environment; and that the individual criminal is merely a reflex of the tendencies of the aggregate.

With the social consciousness wakened, the average individual may learn to refuse the "honor" of being the bloodhound of the law. He may cease to persecute, despise, and mistrust the social offender, and give him a chance to live and breathe among his fellows. Institutions are, of course, harder to reach. They are cold, impenetrable, and cruel; still, with the social consciousness quickened, it might be possible to free the prison victims from the brutality of prison officials, guards, and keepers. Public opinion is a powerful weapon; keepers of human prey, even, are afraid of it. They may be taught a little humanity, especially if they realize that their jobs depend upon it.

But the most important step is to demand for the prisoner the right to work while in prison, with some monetary recompense that would enable him to lay aside a little for the day of his release, the beginning of a new life.

It is almost ridiculous to hope much from present society when we consider that workingmen, wage-slaves themselves, object to convict labor. I shall not go into the cruelty of this objection, but merely consider the impracticability of it. To begin with, the opposition so far raised by organized labor has been directed against windmills. Prisoners have always worked; only the State has been their exploiter, even as the individual employer has been the robber of organized labor. The States have either set the convicts to work for the government, or they have farmed convict labor to private individuals. Twenty-nine of the States pursue the latter plan. The Federal government and seventeen States have discarded it, as have the leading nations of Europe, since it leads to hideous overworking and abuse of prisoners, and to endless graft.

"Rhode Island, the State dominated by Aldrich, offers perhaps the worst example. Under a five-year contract, dated July 7th, 1906, and renewable for five years more at the option of private contractors, the labor of the inmates of the Rhode Island Penitentiary and the Providence County Jail is sold to the Reliance-Sterling Mfg. Co. at the rate of a trifle less than 25 cents a day per man. This Company is really a gigantic Prison Labor Trust, for it also leases the convict labor of Connecticut, Michigan, Indiana, Nebraska, and South Dakota penitentiaries, and the reformatories of New Jersey, Indiana, Illinois, and Wisconsin, eleven establishments in all.

"The enormity of the graft under the Rhode Island contract may be estimated from the fact that this same Company pays 62½ cents a day in Nebraska for the convict's labor, and that Tennessee, for example, gets $1.10 a day for a convict's work from the Gray-Dudley Hardware Co.; Missouri gets 70 cents a day from the Star Overall Mfg. Co.; West Virginia 65 cents a day from the Kraft Mfg. Co., and Maryland 55 cents a day from Oppenheim, Oberndorf & Co., shirt manufacturers. The very difference in prices points to enormous graft. For example, the Reliance-Sterling Mfg. Co. manufactures shirts, the cost by free labor being not less than $1.20 per dozen, while it pays Rhode Island thirty cents a dozen. Furthermore, the State charges this Trust no rent for the use of its huge factory, charges nothing for power, heat, light, or even drainage, and exacts no taxes. What graft!"[47]

It is estimated that more than twelve million dollars' worth of workingmen's shirts and overalls is produced annually in this country by prison labor. It is a woman's industry, and the first reflection that arises is that an immense amount of free female labor is thus displaced. The second consideration is that male convicts, who should be learning trades that would give them some chance of being self-supporting after their release, are kept at this work at which they cannot possibly make a dollar. This is the more serious when we consider that much of this labor is done in reformatories, which so loudly profess to be training their inmates to become useful citizens.

The third, and most important, consideration is that the enormous profits thus wrung from convict labor are a constant incentive to the contractors to exact from their unhappy victims tasks altogether beyond their strength, and to punish them cruelly when their work does not come up to the excessive demands made.

---

47   From the National Committee on Prison Labor.

Another word on the condemnation of convicts to tasks at which they cannot hope to make a living after release. Indiana, for example, is a State that has made a great splurge over being in the front rank of modern penological improvements. Yet, according to the report rendered in 1908 by the training school of its "reformatory," 135 were engaged in the manufacture of chains, 207 in that of shirts; and 255 in the foundry—a total of 597 in three occupations. But at this so-called reformatory 59 occupations were represented by the inmates, 39 of which were connected with country pursuits. Indiana, like other States, professes to be training the inmates of her reformatory to occupations by which they will be able to make their living when released. She actually sets them to work making chains, shirts, and brooms, the latter for the benefit of the Louisville Fancy Grocery Co. Broom-making is a trade largely monopolized by the blind, shirt-making is done by women, and there is only one free chain-factory in the State, and at that a released convict cannot hope to get employment. The whole thing is a cruel farce.

If, then, the States can be instrumental in robbing their helpless victims of such tremendous profits is it not high time for organized labor to stop its idle howl; and to insist on decent remuneration for the convict, even as labor organizations claim for themselves? In that way workingmen would kill the germ which makes of the prisoner an enemy to the interests of labor. I have said elsewhere that thousands of convicts, incompetent and without a trade, without means of subsistence, are yearly turned back into the social fold. These men and women must live, for even an ex-convict has needs. Prison life has made them anti-social beings, and the rigidly closed doors that meet them on their release are not likely to decrease their bitterness. The inevitable result is that they form a favorable nucleus out of which scabs, blacklegs, detectives, and policemen are drawn, only too willing to do the master's bidding. Thus organized labor, by its foolish opposition to work in prison, defeats its own ends. It helps to create poisonous fumes that stifle every attempt for economic betterment. If the workingman wants to avoid these effects, he should *insist* on the right of the convict to work, he should meet him as a brother, take him into his organization, and *with his aid turn against the system which grinds them both.*

Last, but not least, is the growing realization of the barbarity and the inadequacy of the definite sentence. Those who believe in, and earnestly aim at, a change are fast coming to the conclusion that man must be given an opportunity to make good. And how is he to do it with ten, fifteen, or twenty years' imprisonment before him? The hope of liberty and of opportunity is the only incentive to life, especially the prisoner's life. Society has sinned so long against him—it ought at least to leave him that. I am not very sanguine that it will, or that any real change in that direction can take place until the conditions that breed both the prisoner and the jailer will be forever abolished.

Out of his mouth a red, red rose!
Out of his heart a white!
For who can say by what strange way
Christ brings His will to light,
Since the barren staff the pilgrim bore
Bloomed in the great Pope's sight?[48]

---

48 Oscar Wilde, *The Ballad of Reading Gaol.*

MINORITIES VERSUS MAJORITIES

IF I WERE to give a summary of the tendency of our times, I would say, Quantity. The multitude, the mass spirit, dominates everywhere, destroying quality. Our entire life—production, politics, and education—rests on quantity, on numbers. The worker who once took pride—in the thoroughness and quality of his work, has been replaced by brainless, incompetent automatons, who turn out enormous quantities of things, valueless to themselves, and generally injurious to the rest of mankind. Thus quantity, instead of adding to life's comforts and peace, has merely increased man's burden.

In politics, naught but quantity counts. In proportion to its increase, however, principles, ideals, justice, and uprightness are completely swamped by the array of numbers. In the struggle for supremacy the various political parties outdo each other in trickery, deceit, cunning, and shady machinations, confident that the one who succeeds is sure to be hailed by the majority as the victor. That is the only god—Success. As to what expense, what terrible cost to character, is of no moment. We have not far to go in search of proof to verify this sad fact.

Never before did the corruption, the complete rottenness of our government stand so thoroughly exposed; never before were the American people brought face to face with the Judas nature of that political body, which has claimed for years to be absolutely beyond reproach, as the mainstay of our institutions, the true protector of the rights and liberties of the people.

Yet when the crimes of that party became so brazen that even the blind could see them, it needed but to muster up its minions, and its supremacy was assured. Thus the very victims, duped, betrayed, outraged a hundred times, decided, not against, but in favor of the victor. Bewildered, the few asked how could the majority betray the traditions of American liberty? Where was its judgment, its reasoning capacity? That is just it, the majority cannot reason; it has no judgment. Lacking utterly in originality and moral courage, the majority has always placed its destiny in the hands of others. Incapable of standing responsibilities, it has followed its leaders even unto destruction. Dr. Stockman was right: "The most dangerous enemies of truth and justice in our midst are the compact majorities, the damned compact majority." Without ambition or initiative, the compact mass hates nothing so much as innovation. It has always opposed, condemned, and hounded the innovator, the pioneer of a new truth.

The oft repeated slogan of our time is, among all politicians, the Socialists included, that ours is an era of individualism, of the minority. Only those who do not probe beneath the surface might be led to entertain this view. Have not the few accumulated the wealth of the world? Are they not the masters, the absolute kings of the situation? Their success, however, is due not to individualism, but to the inertia, the cravenness, the utter submission of the mass. The latter wants but to be dominated, to be led, to be coerced. As to individualism, at no time in human history did it have less chance of expression, less opportunity to assert itself in a normal, healthy manner.

The individual educator imbued with honesty of purpose, the artist or writer of original ideas, the independent scientist or explorer, the non-compromising pioneers of social changes are daily pushed to the wall by men whose learning and creative ability have become decrepit with age.

Educators of Ferrer's[49] type are nowhere tolerated, while the dietitians of predigested food, à la Professors Eliot and Butler, are the successful perpetuators of an age of nonentities, of automatons. In the literary and dramatic world, the Humphrey Wards and Clyde Fitches are the idols of the mass, while but few know or appreciate the beauty and genius of an Emerson, Thoreau, Whitman; an Ibsen, a Hauptmann, a Butler Yeats, or a Stephen Phillips. They are like solitary stars, far beyond the horizon of the multitude.

Publishers, theatrical managers, and critics ask not for the quality inherent in creative art, but will it meet with a good sale, will it suit the palate of the people? Alas, this palate is like a dumping ground; it relishes anything that needs no mental mastication. As a result, the mediocre, the ordinary, the commonplace represents the chief literary output.

Need I say that in art we are confronted with the same sad facts? One has but to inspect our parks and thoroughfares to realize the hideousness and vulgarity of the art manufacture. Certainly, none but a majority taste would tolerate such an outrage on art. False in conception and barbarous in execution, the statuary that infests American cities has as much relation to true art, as a totem to a Michael Angelo. Yet that is the only art that succeeds. The true artistic genius, who will not cater to accepted notions, who exercises originality, and strives to be true to life, leads an obscure and wretched existence. His work may someday become the fad of the mob, but not until his heart's blood had been exhausted; not until the pathfinder has ceased to be, and a throng of an idealless and visionless mob has done to death the heritage of the master.

It is said that the artist of today cannot create because Prometheus-like he is bound to the rock of economic necessity. This, however, is true of art in all ages. Michael

---

49 Francisco Ferrer (1859–1909), radical freethinker, anarchist, and educationist who founded a network of secular, private libertarian schools in and near Barcelona, Spain.

Angelo was dependent on his patron saint, no less than the sculptor or painter of today, except that the art connoisseurs of those days were far away from the madding crowd. They felt honored to be permitted to worship at the shrine of the master.

The art protector of our time knows but one criterion, one value—the dollar. He is not concerned about the quality of any great work, but in the quantity of dollars his purchase implies. Thus the financier in Mirbeau's *Les affaires sont les affaires*[50] points to some blurred arrangement in colors, saying: "See how great it is; it cost 50,000 francs." Just like our own parvenus. The fabulous figures paid for their great art discoveries must make up for the poverty of their taste.

The most unpardonable sin in society is independence of thought. That this should be so terribly apparent in a country whose symbol is democracy, is very significant of the tremendous power of the majority.

Wendell Phillips said fifty years ago: "In our country of absolute democratic equality, public opinion is not only omnipotent, it is omnipresent. There is no refuge from its tyranny, there is no hiding from its reach, and the result is that if you take the old Greek lantern and go about to seek among a hundred, you will not find a single American who has not, or who does not fancy at least he has, something to gain or lose in his ambition, his social life, or business, from the good opinion and the votes of those around him. And the consequence is that instead of being a mass of individuals, each one fearlessly blurting out his own conviction, as a nation compared to other nations we are a mass of cowards. More than any other people we are afraid of each other."[51] Evidently we have not advanced very far from the condition that confronted Wendell Phillips.

Today, as then, public opinion is the omnipresent tyrant; today, as then, the majority represents a mass of cowards, willing to accept him who mirrors its own soul and mind poverty. That accounts for the unprecedented rise of a man like Roosevelt. He embodies the very worst element of mob psychology. A politician, he knows that the majority cares little for ideals or integrity. What it craves is display. It matters not whether that be a dog show, a prize fight, the lynching of a "nigger," the rounding up of some petty offender, the marriage exposition of an heiress, or the acrobatic stunts of an ex-president. The more hideous the mental contortions, the greater the delight and bravos of the mass. Thus, poor in ideals and vulgar of soul, Roosevelt continues to be the man of the hour.

On the other hand, men towering high above such political pygmies, men of refinement, of culture, of ability, are jeered into silence as mollycoddles. It is absurd to claim that ours is the era of individualism. Ours is merely a more poignant repetition

---

50   Octave Mirbeau (1848–1917) French novelist, journalist, and playwright. His 1903 comedy, *Business is Business* [*Les affaires sont les affaires*] was translated into English in 1905.
51   Wendell Phillips (1811–1884), U.S. American abolitionist, advocate for Indigenous rights, attorney and orator.

of the phenomenon of all history: every effort for progress, for enlightenment, for science, for religious, political, and economic liberty, emanates from the minority, and not from the mass. Today, as ever, the few are misunderstood, hounded, imprisoned, tortured, and killed.

The principle of brotherhood expounded by the agitator of Nazareth preserved the germ of life, of truth and justice, so long as it was the beacon light of the few. The moment the majority seized upon it, that great principle became a shibboleth and harbinger of blood and fire, spreading suffering and disaster. The attack on the omnipotence of Rome, led by the colossal figures of Huss, Calvin, and Luther, was like a sunrise amid the darkness of the night. But so soon as Luther and Calvin turned politicians and began catering to the small potentates, the nobility, and the mob spirit, they jeopardized the great possibilities of the Reformation. They won success and the majority, but that majority proved no less cruel and bloodthirsty in the persecution of thought and reason than was the Catholic monster. Woe to the heretics, to the minority, who would not bow to its dicta. After infinite zeal, endurance, and sacrifice, the human mind is at last free from the religious phantom; the minority has gone on in pursuit of new conquests, and the majority is lagging behind, handicapped by truth grown false with age.

Politically the human race would still be in the most absolute slavery, were it not for the John Balls, the Wat Tylers, the Tells, the innumerable individual giants who fought inch by inch against the power of kings and tyrants. But for individual pioneers the world would have never been shaken to its very roots by that tremendous wave, the French Revolution. Great events are usually preceded by apparently small things. Thus the eloquence and fire of Camille Desmoulins was like the trumpet before Jericho, razing to the ground that emblem of torture, of abuse, of horror, the Bastille.

Always, at every period, the few were the banner bearers of a great idea, of liberating effort. Not so the mass, the leaden weight of which does not let it move. The truth of this is borne out in Russia with greater force than elsewhere. Thousands of lives have already been consumed by that bloody regime, yet the monster on the throne is not appeased. How is such a thing possible when ideas, culture, literature, when the deepest and finest emotions groan under the iron yoke? The majority, that compact, immobile, drowsy mass, the Russian peasant, after a century of struggle, of sacrifice, of untold misery, still believes that the rope which strangles "the man with the white hands" brings luck.

In the American struggle for liberty, the majority was no less of a stumbling block. Until this very day the ideas of Jefferson, of Patrick Henry, of Thomas Paine, are denied and sold by their posterity. The mass wants none of them. The greatness and courage worshipped in Lincoln have been forgotten in the men who created the background for the panorama of that time. The true patron saints of the black men were represented in that handful of fighters in Boston, Lloyd Garrison, Wendell Phillips, Thoreau, Margaret Fuller, and Theodore Parker, whose great courage and sturdiness culminated in that somber giant John Brown. Their untiring zeal, their eloquence and perseverance undermined the stronghold of the Southern lords. Lincoln and his minions followed only when abolition had become a practical issue, recognized as such by all.

About fifty years ago, a meteor-like idea made its appearance on the social horizon of the world, an idea so far-reaching, so revolutionary, so all-embracing as to spread terror in the heart of tyrants everywhere. On the other hand, that idea was a harbinger of joy, of cheer, of hope to the millions. The pioneers knew the difficulties in their way, they knew the opposition, the persecution, the hardships that would meet them, but proud and unafraid they started on their march onward, ever onward. Now that idea has become a popular slogan. Almost everyone is a Socialist today: the rich man, as well as his poor victim; the upholders of law and authority, as well as their unfortunate culprits; the freethinker, as well as the perpetuator of religious falsehoods; the fashionable lady, as well as the shirtwaist girl. Why not? Now that the truth of fifty years ago has become a lie, now that it has been clipped of all its youthful imagination, and been robbed of its vigor, its strength, its revolutionary ideal—why not? Now that it is no longer a beautiful vision, but a "practical, workable scheme," resting on the will of the majority, why not? Political cunning ever sings the praise of the mass: the poor majority, the outraged, the abused, the giant majority, if only it would follow us.

Who has not heard this litany before? Who does not know this never-varying refrain of all politicians? That the mass bleeds, that it is being robbed and exploited, I know as well as our vote-baiters. But I insist that not the handful of parasites, but the mass itself is responsible for this horrible state of affairs. It clings to its masters, loves the whip, and is the first to cry "Crucify!" the moment a protesting voice is raised against the sacredness of capitalistic authority or any other decayed institution. Yet how long would authority and private property exist, if not for the willingness of the mass to become soldiers, policemen, jailers, and hangmen. The Socialist demagogues know that as well as I, but they maintain the myth of the virtues of the majority, because their very scheme of life means the perpetuation of power. And how could the latter be acquired without numbers? Yes, authority, coercion, and dependence rest on the mass, but never freedom or the free unfoldment of the individual, never the birth of a free society.

Not because I do not feel with the oppressed, the disinherited of the earth; not because I do not know the shame, the horror, the indignity of the lives the people lead, do I repudiate the majority as a creative force for good. Oh, no, no! But because I know so well that as a compact mass it has never stood for justice of equality. It has suppressed the human voice, subdued the human spirit, chained the human body.

As a mass its aim has always been to make life uniform, gray, and monotonous as the desert. As a mass it will always be the annihilator of individuality, of free initiative, of originality. I therefore believe with Emerson that "the masses are crude, lame, pernicious in their demands and influence, and need not to be flattered, but to be schooled. I wish not to concede anything to them, but to drill, divide, and break them up, and draw individuals out of them. Masses! The calamity are the masses. I do not wish any mass at all, but honest men only, lovely, sweet, accomplished women only."

In other words, the living, vital truth of social and economic well-being will become a reality only through the zeal, courage, the non-compromising determination of intelligent minorities, and not through the mass.

PATRIOTISM: A MENACE TO LIBERTY

W HAT IS PATRIOTISM? Is it love of one's birthplace, the place of childhood's recollections and hopes, dreams and aspirations? Is it the place where, in childlike naivety, we would watch the fleeting clouds, and wonder why we, too, could not run so swiftly? The place where we would count the milliard glittering stars, ter-ror-stricken lest each one "an eye should be," piercing the very depths of our little souls? Is it the place where we would listen to the music of the birds, and long to have wings to fly, even as they, to distant lands? Or the place where we would sit at mother's knee, enraptured by wonderful tales of great deeds and conquests? In short, is it love for the spot, every inch representing dear and precious recollections of a happy, joyous, and playful childhood?

If that were patriotism, few American men of today could be called upon to be patriotic, since the place of play has been turned into factory, mill, and mine, while deafening sounds of machinery have replaced the music of the birds. Nor can we longer hear the tales of great deeds, for the stories our mothers tell today are but those of sorrow, tears, and grief.

What, then, is patriotism? "Patriotism, sir, is the last resort of scoundrels," said Dr. Johnson. Leo Tolstoy, the greatest anti-patriot of our times, defines patriotism as the principle that will justify the training of wholesale murderers; a trade that requires better equipment for the exercise of man-killing than the making of such necessi-ties of life as shoes, clothing, and houses; a trade that guarantees better returns and greater glory than that of the average workingman.

Gustave Hervé, another great anti-patriot, justly calls patriotism a superstition—one far more injurious, brutal, and inhumane than religion.[52] The superstition of religion originated in man's inability to explain natural phenomena. That is, when primitive man heard thunder or saw the lightning, he could not account for either, and therefore concluded that back of them must be a force greater than himself. Similarly he saw a supernatural force in the rain, and in the various other changes in nature. Patriotism, on the other hand, is a superstition artificially created and maintained through a network of lies and falsehoods; a superstition that robs man of his self-respect and dignity, and increases his arrogance and conceit.

Indeed, conceit, arrogance, and egotism are the essentials of patriotism. Let me

---

52   Gustave Hervé (1871–1944), French politician.

illustrate. Patriotism assumes that our globe is divided into little spots, each one surrounded by an iron gate. Those who have had the fortune of being born on some particular spot, consider themselves better, nobler, grander, more intelligent than the living beings inhabiting any other spot. It is, therefore, the duty of everyone living on that chosen spot to fight, kill, and die in the attempt to impose his superiority upon all the others.

The inhabitants of the other spots reason in like manner, of course, with the result that, from early infancy, the mind of the child is poisoned with blood-curdling stories about the Germans, the French, the Italians, Russians, etc. When the child has reached manhood, he is thoroughly saturated with the belief that he is chosen by the Lord himself to depend his country against the attack or invasion of any foreigner. It is for that purpose that we are clamoring for a greater army and navy, more battleships and ammunition. It is for that purpose that America has within a short time spent four hundred million dollars. Just think of it—four hundred million dollars taken from the produce of *the people*. For surely it is not the rich who contribute to patriotism. They are cosmopolitans, perfectly at home in every land. We in America know well the truth of this. Are not our rich Americans Frenchmen in France, Germans in Germany, or Englishmen in England? And do they not squander with cosmopolitan grace fortunes coined by American factory children and cotton slaves? Yes, theirs is the patriotism that will make it possible to send messages of condolence to a despot like the Russian Tsar, when any mishap befalls him, as President Roosevelt did in the name of *his* people, when Sergius was punished by the Russian revolutionists.

It is a patriotism that will assist the arch-murderer, Diaz, in destroying thousands of lives in Mexico, or that will even aid in arresting Mexican revolutionists on American soil and keep them incarcerated in American prisons, without the slightest cause or reason.

But, then, patriotism is not for those who represent wealth and powder. It is good enough for the people. It reminds one of the historic wisdom of Frederick the Great, the bosom friend of Voltaire, who said: "Religion is a fraud, but it must be maintained for the masses."

That patriotism is rather a costly institution, no one will doubt after considering the following statistics. The progressive increase of the expenditures for the leading armies and navies of the world during the last quarter of a century is a fact of such gravity as to startle every thoughtful student of economic problem. It may be briefly indicated by dividing the time from 1881 to 1905 into five-year periods, and noting the disbursements of several great nations for army and navy purposes during the first and last of those periods. From the first to the last of the periods noted the expenditures of Great Britain increased from $2,101,848,936 to $4,143,226,885, those of France from $3,324,500,000 to $3,455,109,900, those of Germany from $725,000,200 to $2,700,375,600, those of the United States from $1,275,500,750 to

$2,650,900,450, those of Russia from $1,900,975,500 to $5,250,445,100, those of Italy from $1,600,975,750 to $1,755,500,100, and those of Japan from $182,900,500 to $700,925,475.[53]

The military expenditures of each of the nations mentioned increased in each of the five-year periods under review. During the entire interval from 1881 to 1905 Great Britain's outlay for her army increased fourfold, that of the United States was tripled, Russia's was doubled, that of Germany increased 35 percent, that of France about 15 percent, and that of Japan nearly 500 percent. If we compare the expenditures of these nations upon their armies with their total expenditures for all the twenty-five years ending with 1905, the proportion rose as follows:

In Great Britain from 20 percent to 37; in the United States from 15 to 23; in France from 16 to 18; in Italy from 12 to 15; in Japan from 12 to 14. On the other hand, it is interesting to note that the proportion in Germany decreased from about 58 percent to 25, the decrease being due to the enormous increase in the imperial expenditures for other purposes, the fact being that the army expenditures for the period of 1901–5 were higher than for any five-year period preceding. Statistics show that the countries in which army expenditures are greatest, in proportion to the total national revenues, are Great Britain, the United States, Japan, France, and Italy, in the order named.

The showing as to the cost of great navies is equally impressive. During the twenty-five years ending with 1905 naval expenditures increased approximately as follows: Great Britain, 300 percent; France 60 percent; Germany 600 percent; the United States 525 percent; Russia 300 percent; Italy 250 percent; and Japan, 700 percent. With the exception of Great Britain, the United States spends more for naval purposes than any other nation, and this expenditure bears also a larger proportion to the entire national disbursements than that of any other power. In the period 1881–5, the expenditure for the United States navy was $6.20 out of each $100 appropriated for all national purposes; the amount rose to $6.60 for the next five-year period, to $8.10 for the next, to $11.70 for the next, and to $16.40 for 1901–5. It is morally certain that the outlay for the current period of five years will show a still further increase.

The rising cost of militarism may be still further illustrated by computing it as a per capita tax on population. From the first to the last of the five-year periods taken as the basis for the comparisons here given, it has risen as follows: In Great Britain, from $18.47 to $52.50; in France, from $19.66 to $23.62; in Germany, from $10.17 to $15.51; in the United States, from $5.62 to $13.64; in Russia, from $6.14 to $8.37; in Italy, from $9.59 to $11.24, and in Japan from 86 cents to $3.11.

It is in connection with this rough estimate of cost per capita that the economic

---

53   For context, $1,000,000,000 in 1905 is equivalent to $33,667,727,272 and $10 in 1905 is equivalent to $336 in 2022 U.S. dollars.

burden of militarism is most appreciable. The irresistible conclusion from available data is that the increase of expenditure for army and navy purposes is rapidly surpassing the growth of population in each of the countries considered in the present calculation. In other words, a continuation of the increased demands of militarism threatens each of those nations with a progressive exhaustion both of men and resources.

The awful waste that patriotism necessitates ought to be sufficient to cure the man of even average intelligence from this disease. Yet patriotism demands still more. The people are urged to be patriotic and for that luxury they pay, not only by supporting their "defenders," but even by sacrificing their own children. Patriotism requires allegiance to the flag, which means obedience and readiness to kill father, mother, brother, sister.

The usual contention is that we need a standing army to protect the country from foreign invasion. Every intelligent man and woman knows, however, that this is a myth maintained to frighten and coerce the foolish. The governments of the world, knowing each other's interests, do not invade each other. They have learned that they can gain much more by international arbitration of disputes than by war and conquest. Indeed, as Carlyle said, "War is a quarrel between two thieves too cowardly to fight their own battle; therefore they take boys from one village and another village, stick them into uniforms, equip them with guns, and let them loose like wild beasts against each other."

It does not require much wisdom to trace every war back to a similar cause. Let us take our own Spanish-American war, supposedly a great and patriotic event in the history of the United States. How our hearts burned with indignation against the atrocious Spaniards! True, our indignation did not flare up spontaneously. It was nurtured by months of newspaper agitation, and long after Butcher Weyler had killed off many noble Cubans and outraged many Cuban women. Still, in justice to the American Nation be it said, it did grow indignant and was willing to fight, and that it fought bravely. But when the smoke was over, the dead buried, and the cost of the war came back to the people in an increase in the price of commodities and rent—that is, when we sobered up from our patriotic spree—it suddenly dawned on us that the cause of the Spanish-American war was the consideration of the price of sugar; or, to be more explicit, that the lives, blood, and money of the American people were used to protect the interests of American capitalists, which were threatened by the Spanish government. That this is not an exaggeration, but is based on absolute facts and figures, is best proven by the attitude of the American government to Cuban labor. When Cuba was firmly in the clutches of the United States, the very soldiers sent to liberate Cuba were ordered to shoot Cuban workingmen during the great cigarmakers' strike, which took place shortly after the war.

Nor do we stand alone in waging war for such causes. The curtain is beginning to be lifted on the motives of the terrible Russo-Japanese war, which cost so much blood and tears. And we see again that back of the fierce Moloch of war stands the still fiercer god of Commercialism. Kuropatkin, the Russian Minister of War during the Russo-Japanese struggle, has revealed the true secret behind the latter. The Tsar and his Grand Dukes, having invested money in Korean concessions, the war was forced for the sole purpose of speedily accumulating large fortunes.

The contention that a standing army and navy is the best security of peace is about as logical as the claim that the most peaceful citizen is he who goes about heavily armed. The experience of every-day life fully proves that the armed individual is invariably anxious to try his strength. The same is historically true of governments. Really peaceful countries do not waste life and energy in war preparations, with the result that peace is maintained.

However, the clamor for an increased army and navy is not due to any foreign danger. It is owing to the dread of the growing discontent of the masses and of the international spirit among the workers. It is to meet the internal enemy that the Powers of various countries are preparing themselves; an enemy, who, once awakened to consciousness, will prove more dangerous than any foreign invader.

The powers that have for centuries been engaged in enslaving the masses have made a thorough study of their psychology. They know that the people at large are like children whose despair, sorrow, and tears can be turned into joy with a little toy. And the more gorgeously the toy is dressed, the louder the colors, the more it will appeal to the million-headed child.

An army and navy represents the people's toys. To make them more attractive and acceptable, hundreds and thousands of dollars are being spent for the display of these toys. That was the purpose of the American government in equipping a fleet and sending it along the Pacific coast, that every American citizen should be made to feel the pride and glory of the United States. The city of San Francisco spent one hundred thousand dollars for the entertainment of the feet; Los Angeles, sixty thousand; Seattle and Tacoma, about one hundred thousand. To entertain the fleet, did I say? To dine and wine a few superior officers, while the "brave boys" had to mutiny to get sufficient food. Yes, two hundred and sixty thousand dollars were spent on fireworks, theatre parties, arid revelries, at a time when men, women, and children through the breadth and length of the country were starving in the streets; when thousands of unemployed were ready to sell their labor at any price.

Two hundred and sixty thousand dollars! What could not have been accomplished with such an enormous sum? But instead of bread and shelter, the children of those cities were taken to see the fleet, that it may remain, as one of the newspapers said, "a lasting memory for the child."

A wonderful thing to remember, is it not? The implements of civilized slaughter. If the mind of the child is to be poisoned with such memories, what hope is there for a true realization of human brotherhood?

We Americans claim to be a peace-loving people. We hate bloodshed; we are opposed to violence. Yet we go into spasms of joy over the possibility of projecting dynamite bombs from flying machines upon helpless citizens. We are ready to hang, electrocute, or lynch anyone, who, from economic necessity, will risk his own life in the attempt upon that of some industrial magnate. Yet our hearts swell with pride at the thought that America is becoming the most powerful nation on earth, and that it will eventually plant her iron foot on the necks of all other nations.

Such is the logic of patriotism.

Considering the evil results that patriotism is fraught with for the average man, it is as nothing compared with the insult and injury that patriotism heaps upon the soldier himself,—that poor, deluded victim of superstition and ignorance. He, the savior of his country, the protector of his nation,—what has patriotism in store for him? A life of slavish submission, vice, and perversion, during peace; a life of danger, exposure, and death, during war.

While on a recent lecture tour in San Francisco, I visited the Presidio, the most beautiful spot overlooking the Bay and Golden Gate Park. Its purpose should have been playgrounds for children, gardens and music for the recreation of the weary. Instead it is made ugly, dull, and gray by barracks,—barracks wherein the rich would not allow their dogs to dwell. In these miserable shanties soldiers are herded like cattle; here they waste their young days, polishing the boots and brass buttons of their superior officers. Here, too, I saw the distinction of classes: sturdy sons of a free Republic, drawn up in line like convicts, saluting every passing shrimp of a lieutenant. American equality, degrading manhood and elevating the uniform!

Barrack life further tends to develop tendencies of sexual perversion. It is gradually producing along this line results similar to European military conditions. Havelock Ellis, the noted writer on sex psychology, has made a thorough study of the subject. I quote: "Some of the barracks are great centers of male prostitution.... The number of soldiers who prostitute themselves is greater than we are willing to believe. It is no exaggeration to say that in certain regiments the presumption is in favor of the venality of the majority of the men....On summer evenings Hyde Park and the neighborhood of Albert Gate are full of guardsmen and others plying a lively trade, and with little disguise, in uniform or out....In most cases the proceeds form a comfortable addition to Tommy Atkins' pocket money."

To what extent this perversion has eaten its way into the army and navy can best be judged from the fact that special houses exist for this form of prostitution. The practice is not limited to England; it is universal. "Soldiers are no less sought after in France than in England or in Germany, and special houses for military prostitution exist both in Paris and the garrison towns."

Had Mr. Havelock Ellis included America in his investigation of sex perversion, he would have found that the same conditions prevail in our army and navy as in those of other countries. The growth of the standing army inevitably adds to the spread of sex perversion; the barracks are the incubators.

Aside from the sexual effects of barrack life, it also tends to unfit the soldier for useful labor after leaving the army. Men, skilled in a trade, seldom enter the army or navy, but even they, after a military experience, find themselves totally unfitted for their former occupations. Having acquired habits of idleness and a taste for excitement and adventure, no peaceful pursuit can content them. Released from the army, they can turn to no useful work. But it is usually the social riff-raff, discharged prisoners and the like, whom either the struggle for life or their own inclination drives into the ranks. These, their military term over, again turn to their former life of crime, more brutalized and degraded than before. It is a well-known fact that in our prisons there is a goodly number of ex-soldiers; while, on the other hand, the army and navy are to a great extent supplied with ex-convicts.

Of all the evil results I have just described none seems to me so detrimental to human integrity as the spirit patriotism has produced in the case of Private William Buwalda.[54] Because he foolishly believed that one can be a soldier and exercise his rights as a man at the same time, the military authorities punished him severely. True, he had served his country fifteen years, during which time his record was unimpeachable. According to Gen. Funston, who reduced Buwalda's sentence to three years, "the first duty of an officer or an enlisted man is unquestioned obedience and loyalty to the government, and it makes no difference whether he approves of that government or not." Thus Funston stamps the true character of allegiance. According to him, entrance into the army abrogates the principles of the Declaration of Independence.

What a strange development of patriotism that turns a thinking being into a loyal machine!

In justification of this most outrageous sentence of Buwalda, Gen. Funston tells the American people that the soldier's action was "a serious crime equal to treason." Now, what did this "terrible crime" really consist of? Simply in this: William Buwalda was one of fifteen hundred people who attended a public meeting in San Francisco; and, oh, horrors, he shook hands with the speaker, Emma Goldman. A terrible crime, indeed, which the General calls "a great military offense, infinitely worse than desertion."

Can there be a greater indictment against patriotism than that it will thus brand a man a criminal, throw him into prison, and rob him of the results of fifteen years of faithful service?

Buwalda gave to his country the best years of his life and his very manhood. But all that was as nothing. Patriotism is inexorable and, like all insatiable monsters,

---

54   See note 1 above.

demands all or nothing. It does not admit that a soldier is also a human being, who has a right to his own feelings and opinions, his own inclinations and ideas. No, patriotism cannot admit of that. That is the lesson which Buwalda was made to learn; made to learn at a rather costly, though not at a useless price. When he returned to freedom, he had lost his position in the army, but he regained his self-respect. After all, that is worth three years of imprisonment.

A writer on the military conditions of America, in a recent article, commented on the power of the military man over the civilian in Germany. He said, among other things, that if our Republic had no other meaning than to guarantee all citizens equal rights, it would have just cause for existence. I am convinced that the writer was not in Colorado during the patriotic régime of General Bell. He probably would have changed his mind had he seen how, in the name of patriotism and the Republic, men were thrown into bull-pens, dragged about, driven across the border, and subjected to all kinds of indignities. Nor is that Colorado incident the only one in the growth of military power in the United States. There is hardly a strike where troops and militia do not come to the rescue of those in power, and where they do not act as arrogantly and brutally as do the men wearing the Kaiser's uniform. Then, too, we have the Dick military law. Had the writer forgotten that?

A great misfortune with most of our writers is that they are absolutely ignorant on current events, or that, lacking honesty, they will not speak of these matters. And so it has come to pass that the Dick military law was rushed through Congress with little discussion and still less publicity,—a law which gives the President the power to turn a peaceful citizen into a bloodthirsty man-killer, supposedly for the defense of the country, in reality for the protection of the interests of that particular party whose mouthpiece the President happens to be.

Our writer claims that militarism can never become such a power in America as abroad, since it is voluntary with us, while compulsory in the Old World. Two very important facts, however, the gentleman forgets to consider. First, that conscription has created in Europe a deep-seated hatred of militarism among all classes of society. Thousands of young recruits enlist under protest and, once in the army, they will use every possible means to desert. Second, that it is the compulsory feature of militarism which has created a tremendous anti-militarist movement, feared by European Powers far more than anything else. After all, the greatest bulwark of capitalism is militarism. The very moment the latter is undermined, capitalism will totter. True, we have no conscription; that is, men are not usually forced to enlist in the army, but we have developed a far more exacting and rigid force—necessity. Is it not a fact that during industrial depressions there is a tremendous increase in the number of enlistments? The trade of militarism may not be either lucrative or honorable, but it is better than tramping the country in search of work, standing in the bread line, or sleeping in municipal lodging houses. After all, it means thirteen dollars per month, three meals a day, and a place to sleep. Yet even necessity is not sufficiently strong a factor to bring into the army an element of character and manhood. No wonder our military authorities complain of the "poor material" enlisting in the army and navy. This admission is a very encouraging sign. It proves that there is still enough of the spirit of independence and love of liberty left in the average American to risk starvation rather than don the uniform.

Thinking men and women the world over are beginning to realize that patriotism is too narrow and limited a conception to meet the necessities of our time. The centralization of power has brought into being an international feeling of solidarity among the oppressed nations of the world; a solidarity which represents a greater harmony of interests between the workingman of America and his brothers abroad than between the American miner and his exploiting compatriot; a solidarity which fears not foreign invasion, because it is bringing all the workers to the point when they will say to their masters, "Go and do your own killing. We have done it long enough for you."

This solidarity is awakening the consciousness of even the soldiers, they, too, being flesh of the flesh of the great human family. A solidarity that has proven infallible more than once during past struggles, and which has been the impetus inducing the Parisian soldiers, during the Commune of 1871,[55] to refuse to obey when ordered to shoot their brothers. It has given courage to the men who mutinied on Russian warships during recent years. It will eventually bring about the uprising of all the oppressed and downtrodden against their international exploiters.

The proletariat of Europe has realized the great force of that solidarity and has, as a result, inaugurated a war against patriotism and its bloody specter, militarism. Thousands of men fill the prisons of France, Germany, Russia, and the Scandinavian countries, because they dared to defy the ancient superstition. Nor is the movement limited to the working class; it has embraced representatives in all stations of life, its chief exponents being men and women prominent in art, science, and letters.

America will have to follow suit. The spirit of militarism has already permeated all walks of life. Indeed, I am convinced that militarism is growing a greater danger here than anywhere else, because of the many bribes capitalism holds out to those whom it wishes to destroy.

The beginning has already been made in the schools. Evidently the government holds to the Jesuitical conception, "Give me the child mind, and I will mold the man." Children are trained in military tactics, the glory of military achievements extolled in the curriculum, and the youthful minds perverted to suit the government. Further, the youth of the country is appealed to in glaring posters to join the army and navy. "A fine chance to see the world!" cries the governmental huckster.

---

55 A revolutionary government that seized power in Paris, France, from 18 March to 28 May 1871.

Thus innocent boys are morally shanghaied into patriotism, and the military Moloch strides conquering through the Nation.

The American workingman has suffered so much at the hands of the soldier, State and Federal, that he is quite justified in his disgust with, and his opposition to, the uniformed parasite. However, mere denunciation will not solve this great problem. What we need is a propaganda of education for the soldier: anti-patriotic literature that will enlighten him as to the real horrors of his trade, and that will awaken his consciousness to his true relation to the man to whose labor he owes his very existence.

It is precisely this that the authorities fear most. It is already high treason for a soldier to attend a radical meeting. No doubt they will also stamp it high treason for a soldier to read a radical pamphlet. But, then, has not authority from time immemorial stamped every step of progress as treasonable? Those, however, who earnestly strive for social reconstruction can well afford to face all that; for it is probably even more important to carry the truth into the barracks than into the factory. When we have undermined the patriotic lie, we shall have cleared the path for that great structure wherein all nationalities shall be united into a universal brotherhood,—a truly **FREE SOCIETY**.

INTELLECTUAL PROLETARIANS

THE PROLETARIZATION OF our time reaches far beyond the field of manual labor; indeed, in the larger sense all those who work for their living, whether with hand or brain, all those who must sell their skill, knowledge, experience and ability, are proletarians. From this point of view, our entire system, excepting a very limited class, has been proletarianized.

Our whole social fabric is maintained by the efforts of mental and physical labor. In return for that, the intellectual proletarians, even as the workers in shop and mine, eke out an insecure and pitiful existence, and are more dependent upon the masters than those who work with their hands.

No doubt there is a difference between the yearly income of a Brisbane and a Pennsylvania mine worker. The former, with his colleagues in the newspaper office, in the theater, college and university, may enjoy material comfort and social position, but with it all they are proletarians, inasmuch as they are slavishly dependent upon the Hearsts, the Pulitzers, the Theater Trusts, the publishers and, above all, upon a stupid and vulgar public opinion. This terrible dependence upon those who can make the price and dictate the terms of intellectual activities is more degrading than the position of the worker in any trade. The pathos of it is that those who are engaged in intellectual occupations, no matter how sensitive they might have been in the beginning, grow callous, cynical and indifferent to their degradation. That has certainly happened to Brisbane, whose parents were idealists working with Fourier in the early co-operative ventures. Brisbane, who himself began as a man of ideals, but who has become so enmeshed by material success that he has forsworn and betrayed every principle of his youth.

Naturally so. Success achieved by the most contemptible means cannot but destroy the soul. Yet that is the goal of our day. It helps to cover up the inner corruption and gradually dulls one's scruples, so that those who begin with some high ambition cannot, even if they would, create anything out of themselves.

In other words, those who are placed in positions which demand the surrender of personality, which insist on strict conformity to definite political policies and opinions, must deteriorate, must become mechanical, must lose all capacity to give anything really vital. The world is full of such unfortunate cripples. Their dream is to "arrive," no matter at what cost. If only we would stop to consider what it means to "arrive," we would pity the unfortunate victim. Instead of that, we look to the artist, the poet, the writer, the dramatist and thinker who have "arrived," as the final authority on all matters, whereas in reality their "arrival" is synonymous with mediocrity, with the denial and betrayal of what might in the beginning have meant something real and ideal.

The "arrived" artists are dead souls upon the intellectual horizon. The uncompromising and daring spirits never "arrive." Their life represents an endless battle with the stupidity and the dullness of their time. They must remain what Nietzsche calls "untimely," because everything that strives for new form, new expression or new values is always doomed to be untimely.

The real pioneers in ideas, in art and in literature have remained aliens to their time, misunderstood and repudiated. And if, as in the case of Zola, Ibsen and Tolstoy, they compelled their time to accept them, it was due to their extraordinary genius and even more so to the awakening and seeking of a small minority for new truths, to whom these men were the inspiration and intellectual support. Yet even to this day Ibsen is unpopular, while Poe, Whitman and Strindberg have never "arrived."

The logical conclusion is this: those who will not worship at the shrine of money need not hope for recognition. On the other hand, they will also not have to think other people's thoughts or wear other people's political clothes. They will not have to proclaim as true that which is false, nor praise that as humanitarian which is brutal. I realize that those who have the courage to defy the economic and social whip are among the few, and we have to deal with the many.

Now, it is a fact that the majority of the intellectual proletarians are in the economic treadmill and have less freedom than those who work in the shops or mines. Unlike the latter, they cannot put on overalls and ride the bumpers to the next town in search of a job. In the first place, they have spent a lifetime on a profession, at the expense of all their other faculties. They are therefore unfitted for any other work except the one thing which, parrot-like, they have learned to repeat. We all know how cruelly difficult it is to find a job in any given trade. But to come to a new town without connections and find a position as teacher, writer, musician, bookkeeper, actress or nurse is almost impossible.

If, however, the intellectual proletarian has connections, he must come to them in a presentable shape; he must keep up appearances. And that requires means, of which most professional people have as little as the workers, because even in their "good times" they rarely earn enough to make ends meet.

Then there are the traditions, the habits of the intellectual proletarians, the fact that they must live in a certain district, that they must have certain comforts, that they must buy clothes of a certain quality. All that has emasculated them, has made them unfit for the stress and strain of the life of the bohemian. If he and she drink coffee at night, they cannot sleep. If they stay up a little later than usual, they are

unfitted for the next day's work. In short, they have no vitality and cannot, like the manual worker, meet the hardships of the road. Therefore they are tied in a thousand ways to the most galling, humiliating conditions. But so blind are they to their own lot that they consider themselves superior, better, and more fortunate than their fellow-comrades in the ranks of labor.

Then, too, there are the women who boast of their wonderful economic achievements, and that they can now be self-supporting. Every year our schools and colleges turn out thousands of competitors in the intellectual market, and everywhere the supply is greater than the demand. In order to exist, they must cringe and crawl and beg for a position. Professional women crowd the offices, sit around for hours, grow weary and faint with the search for employment, and yet deceive themselves with the delusion that they are superior to the working girl, or that they are economically independent.

The years of their youth are swallowed up in the acquisition of a profession, in the end to be dependent upon the board of education, the city editor, the publisher or the theatrical manager. The emancipated woman runs away from a stifling home atmosphere, only to rush from employment bureau to the literary broker, and back again. She points with moral disgust to the girl of the redlight district, and is not aware that she too must sing, dance, write or play, and otherwise sell herself a thousand times in return for her living. Indeed, the only difference between the working girl and the intellectual female or male proletarian is a matter of four hours. At 5 A.M. the former stands in line waiting to be called to the job and often face to face with a sign, "No hands wanted." At 9 A.M. the professional woman must face the sign, "No brains wanted."

Under such a state of affairs, what becomes of the high mission of the intellectuals, the poets, the writers, the composers and what not? What are they doing to cut loose from their chains, and how dare they boast that they are helping the masses? Yet you know that they are engaged in uplift work. What a farce! They, so pitiful and low in their slavery themselves, so dependent and helpless! The truth is, the people have nothing to learn from this class of intellectuals, while they have everything to give to them. If only the intellectuals would come down from their lofty pedestal and realize how closely related they are to the people! But they will not do that, not even the radical and liberal intellectuals.

Within the last ten years the intellectual proletarians of advanced tendencies have entered every radical movement. They could, if they would, be of tremendous importance to the workers. But so far they have remained without clarity of vision, without depth of conviction, and without real daring to face the world. It is not because they do not feel deeply the mind- and soul-destroying effects of compromise, or that they do not know the corruption, the degradation in our social, political, business, and family life. Talk to them in private gatherings, or when you get them alone, and they will admit that there isn't a single institution worth preserving. But only privately. Publicly they continue in the same rut as their conservative colleagues. They write the stuff that will sell, and do not go an inch farther than public taste will permit. They speak their thoughts, careful not to offend anyone, and live according to the most stupid conventions of the day. Thus we find men in the legal profession, intellectually emancipated from the belief in government, yet looking to the fleshpots of a judgeship; men who know the corruption of politics, yet belonging to political parties and championing Mr. Roosevelt. Men who realize the prostitution of mind in the newspaper profession, yet holding responsible positions therein. Women who deeply feel the fetters of the marital institution and the indignity of our moral precepts, who yet submit to both; who either stifle their nature or have clandestine relations—but God forbid they should face the world and say, "Mind your own damned business!"

Even in their sympathies for labor—and some of them have genuine sympathies—the intellectual proletarians do not cease to be middle-class, respectable and aloof. This may seem sweeping and unfair, but those who know the various groups will understand that I am not exaggerating. Women of every profession have flocked to Lawrence, to Little Falls, to Paterson, and to the strike districts in this city. Partly out of curiosity, often out of interest. But always they have remained rooted to their middle-class traditions. Always they have deceived themselves and the workers with the notion that they must give the strike respectable prestige, to help the cause.

In the shirtwaistmakers' strike professional women were told to rig themselves out in their best furs and most expensive jewelry, if they wanted to help the girls. Is it necessary to say that while scores of girls were manhandled and brutally hustled into the patrol wagons, the well-dressed pickets were treated with deference and allowed to go home? Thus they had their excitement, and only hurt the cause of labor.

The police are indeed stupid, but not so stupid as not to know the difference in the danger to themselves and their masters from those who are driven to strike by necessity, and those who go into the strike for pastime or "copy." This difference doesn't come from the degree of feeling, nor even the cut of clothes, but from the degree of incentive and courage; and those who still compromise with appearances have no courage.

The police, the courts, the prison authorities and the newspaper owners know perfectly well that the liberal intellectuals, even as the conservatives, are slaves to appearances. That is why their muckraking, their investigations, their sympathies with the workers are never taken seriously. Indeed, they are welcomed by the press, because the reading public loves sensation, hence the muckraker represents a good investment for the concern and for himself. But as far as danger to the ruling class is concerned, it is like the babbling of an infant.

Mr. Sinclair would have died in obscurity but for *The Jungle*, which didn't move a hair upon the heads of the Armours, but netted the author a large sum and a reputation. He may now write the most stupid stuff, sure of finding a market. Yet there is not a workingman anywhere so cringing before respectability as Mr. Sinclair.

Mr. Kibbe Turner would have remained a penny-a-liner but for our political mud-slingers, who used him to make capital against Tammany Hall. Yet the poorest-paid laborer is more independent than Mr. Turner, and certainly more honest than he.

Mr. Hillquit would have remained the struggling revolutionist I knew him twenty-four years ago, but for the workers who helped him to his legal success. Yet there is not a single Russian worker on the East Side so thoroughly bound to respectability and public opinion as Mr. Hillquit.

I could go on indefinitely proving that, though the intellectuals are really proletarians, they are so steeped in middle-class traditions and conventions, so tied and gagged by them, that they dare not move a step.

The cause of it is, I believe, to be sought in the fact that the intellectuals of America have not yet discovered their relation to the workers, to the revolutionary elements which at all times and in every country have been the inspiration of men and women who worked with their brains. They seem to think that they and not the workers represent the creators of culture. But that is a disastrous mistake, as proved in all countries. Only when the intellectual forces of Europe had made common cause with the struggling masses, when they came close to the depths of society, did they give to the world a real culture.

With us, this depth in the minds of our intellectuals is only a place for slumming, for newspaper copy, or on a very rare occasion for a little theoretic sympathy. Never was the latter strong or deep enough to pull them out of themselves, or make them break with their traditions and surroundings. Strikes, conflicts, the use of dynamite, or the efforts of the I.W.W. are exciting to our intellectual proletarians, but after all very foolish when considered in the light of the logical, cool-headed observer. Of course they feel with the I.W.W. man when he is beaten and brutally treated, or with the McNamaras, who cleared the horizon from the foggy belief that in America no one needed use violence. The intellectuals gall too much under their own dependence not to sympathize in such a case. But the sympathy is never strong enough to establish a bond, a solidarity between him and the disinherited. It is the sympathy of aloofness, of experiment.

In other words, it is a theoretic sympathy which all those have who still enjoy a certain amount of comfort and therefore do not see why anyone should break into a fashionable restaurant. It is the kind of sympathy Mrs. Belmont has when she goes to night courts. Or the sympathy of the Osbornes, Dottys and Watsons when they had themselves locked up in prison for a few days. The sympathy of the millionaire Socialist who speaks of "economic determinism."

The intellectual proletarians who are radical and liberal are still so much of the bourgeois régime that their sympathy with the workers is dilettante and does not go farther than the parlor, the so-called salon, or Greenwich Village. It may in a measure be compared to the early period of the awakening of the Russian intellectuals described by Turgenev in *Fathers and Sons*.

The intellectuals of that time, while never so superficial as those I am talking about, indulged in revolutionary ideas, split hairs through the early morning hours, philosophized about all sorts of questions and carried their superior wisdom to the people with their feet deeply rooted in the old. Of course they failed. They were indignant with Turgenev and considered him a traitor to Russia. But he was right. Only when the Russian intellectuals completely broke with their traditions; only when they fully realized that society rests upon a lie, and that they must give themselves to the new completely and unreservedly, did they become a forceful factor in the life of the people. The Kropotkins, the Perovskayas, the Breshkovskayas, and hosts of others repudiated wealth and station and refused to serve King Mammon. They went among the people, not to lift them up but themselves to be lifted up, to be instructed, and in return to give themselves wholly to the people. That accounts for the heroism, the art, the literature of Russia, the unity between the people, the mujik and the intellectual. That to some extent explains the literature of all European countries, the fact that the Strindbergs, the Hauptmanns, the Wedekinds, the Brieux, the Mirbeaus, the Steinlins and Rodins have never dissociated themselves from the people.

Will that ever come to pass in America? Will the American intellectual proletarians ever love the ideal more than their comforts, ever be willing to give up external success for the sake of the vital issues of life? I think so, and that for two reasons. First, the proletarization of the intellectuals will compel them to come closer to labor. Secondly, because of the rigid régime of puritanism, which is causing a tremendous reaction against conventions and narrow moral ties. Struggling artists, writers and dramatists who strive to create something worthwhile aid in breaking down dominant conventions; scores of women who wish to live their lives are helping to undermine our morality of today in their proud defiance of the rules of Mrs. Grundy. Alone they cannot accomplish much. They need the bold indifference and courage of the revolutionary workers, who have broken with all the old rubbish. It is therefore through the co-operation of the intellectual proletarians, who try to find expression, and the revolutionary proletarians who seek to remold life, that we in America will establish a real unity and by means of it wage a successful war against present society.

NELLY BLY INTERVIEW OF EMMA GOLDMAN

Interview in the *New York World,* September 17, 1893
Nelly Bly Again
She Interviews Emma Goldman and Other Anarchists[56]

Do you need an introduction to Emma Goldman? You have seen supposed pictures of her. You have read of her as a property-destroying, capitalist-killing, riot-promoting agitator. You see her in your mind a great raw-boned creature, with short hair and bloomers, a red flag in one hand, a burning torch in the other; both feet constantly off of the ground and "murder!' continually upon her lips.

The was my ideal of her, I confess, and when the matron stood before me saying, "This is Emma Goldman," I gasped in surprise and then laughed.

A little bit of a girl, just 5 feet high, including her boot heels, not showing her 120 pounds; with a saucy, turned-up nose and very expressive blue-gray eyes that gazed inquiringly at me through shell-rimmed glasses was Emma Goldman!

Her quiet little hands held rolled a recent copy of the *Illustrated American.* The modest blue serge Eton suit, with a blue muslin shirtwaist and scarf, had no suggestion of bloomers, and the light brown hair, not banged but falling loosely over the forehead and gathered in a little knot behind, was very pretty and girlish.

The little feet were decorously upon the floor, and the rather full lips parted, showing strong white teeth within, a mild, pleasant voice, with a very fetching accent, said not "murder," but—

"What is it you wish, madam?"

I told her. I sat down beside her, and we talked for two hours.

"I do not want anything published about me," she said, "because people misjudge and exaggerate, and, besides, I do not think it looks well for me to say anything while I am in jail."

"But I want to know something about your former life; how you became an

---

56 Nelly Bly (pen name of Elizabeth Cochran Seaman; 1864–1922) was a pioneering journalist credited with launching a new kind of investigative journalism. She is considered one of the first women to enter the journalist mainstream in the twentieth century. In her day she was most known for her record-breaking trip around the world in seventy-two days and her exposé on a mental institution.

Anarchist, what your theories are, and how you mean to establish them."

She Tells Her Age.

She smiled at me, rather amused, but the smile was a very becoming one, lighting up the gravity of her face and making her look more girlish than ever.

"How old are you?" I asked as a beginning.

"Twenty-five last June," she replied without the faintest hesitancy.

What greater proof do I need that she is an unusual and extraordinary woman?

"But the month of roses has not brought many into my life," she added, with a little smile.

"When did you become an Anarchist, and what made you one?"

"Oh, I have been one all my life, but I never really entered into the work until after the Chicago riot, seven years ago."

"Why are you one?" I asked. "What is your object? What did you hope to gain?"

She smiled again, and slowly smoothed the book upon her knee.

"We are all egotists," she answered. "There are some that, if asked why they are Anarchists, will say, 'for the good of the people.' It is not true, and I do not say it. I am an Anarchist because I am a egotist. It pains me to see others suffer. I cannot bear it. I never hurt a man in my life, and I don't think I could. So, because what others suffer makes me suffer, I am an Anarchist and give my life for the cause, for only through it can be ended all suffering and want and unhappiness.

A Word About Capitalists.

"Everything wrong, crime and sickness and all that, is the result of the system under which we live," she continued earnestly. "Were there no money, and as a result, no capitalists, people would not be over-worked, starved and illy housed, all of which makes them old before their time, diseases them and makes them criminals. To save a dollar the capitalists build their railroads poorly, and along comes a train, and loads of people are killed. What are their lies to him if by their sacrifice he has saved money? But those deaths mean misery, want and crime in many, many families. According to Anarchistic principles, we build the best of railroads, so there shall be no accidents. There is the Broadway cable, for instance. Instead of running a few cars at a frightful speed, in order to save a larger expense, we should run many cars at slow speed, and so have no accidents."

"If you do away with money and employers, who will work upon your railroads?" I asked.

"Those that care for that kind of work. Then everyone shall do that which he likes best, not merely a thing he is compelled to do to earn his daily bread."

"What will you do with the lazy ones, who would not work?"

"No one is lazy. They grow hopeless from the misery of their present existence, and give up. Under our order of things, every men would do the work he liked, and would have as much as his neighbor, so could not be unhappy and discouraged."

"What will you do with your criminals if everyone is free and prisons unheard of?"

Why Are There Criminals?

She smiles, sadly.

"The subject takes a lifetime of study," she answered, "but we believe that we would not have a criminal. Why are there criminals today. Because some have everything, others nothing. Under our system it would be every man equal. The Bible says, 'Thou shalt not steal.' Now, to steal, it is granted, there must be something to steal. We do not grant that there is anything to steal, for everything should be free."

"Do you believe in God, Miss Goldman?"

"Once I did. Until I was seventeen I was very devout, and all my people are so, even today. But when I began to read and study, I lost that belief. I believe in nature, nothing else."

"Where were you born?"

"I was born in Russia and afterwards my family removed to Germany. Although my people were of a good family, I was always in deep sympathy for the poor. I did not think of being an Anarchist then, but I was always trying to see some way to benefit the working classes. I was taught a trade. My father thought that no difference what one's position was, one should master a trade, so I learned dressmaking at a French school. I have worked at this for years, sometimes in my own rooms, and again in establishments."

She Likes to Bathe and Dress.

"Do you care for dress at all?"

"I know that the right of free speech was once guaranteed to every man and woman in this land."

"Oh, of course," she answered, laughing. "I like to look well, but I don't like very fussy dresses. I like my dresses to be plain and quiet, and, above all things," here she laughed as if recalling the oft-declaration of Anarchists' hatred for soap, "I love my bath. I must be clean. Being a German, I was taught cleanliness with my youth, and I do not care how poor my room or my clothes are so long as they are clean."

"What did you do with the money you earned by sewing?"

"Spent it all on books," she said emphatically. "I kept myself in poverty buying books. I have a library of nearly three hundred volumes, and so long as I had something to read I did not mind hunger or shabby clothes."

Think of that you girls who put every dollar upon your backs! Can you not testify to this woman's earnestness of purpose when she sacrifices her looks for books?

Miss Goldman speaks Russian, German, French and English, and reads and writes Spanish and Italian.

Her Ideas of Marriage.

"There is something else I must ask you. We look upon marriage as the foundation of everything that is good. We base everything upon it. You do not believe in marriage. What do you propose shall take its place?"

"I was married," she said, with a little sigh, "when I was scarcely seventeen. I suffered—let me say no more about that. I believe in the marriage of affection. That is the only true marriage. If two people care for each other they have a right to live together so long as that love exists. When it is dead what base immorality for them still to keep together! Oh, I tell you the marriage ceremony is a terrible thing!

"Tell me," she added very seriously, "how can a woman go before a minister and take an oath to love 'this man' all her life? How can she tell but tomorrow, next week, she may get to know this man and hate him. Love is founded on respect, and a woman cannot tell what a man is until she lives with him. Instead of being free to end the relation when her feelings change, she lives on in a state that is the most depraved of all.

"Take the woman who marries for a home and for fine clothes. She goes to the man with a lie on her lips. Still"—with a little uplifting of the hands—"she will not let her skirts touch the poor unfortunate upon the street who deceives no man, but is to him just what she appears! Do away with marriage. Let there be nothing but voluntary affection and there ceases to exist the prostitute wife and the prostitute street woman."

"But the children? What would you do with them? Men would desert; women and children would be left uncared for and destitute," I protested.

"On the contrary, then men would never desert, and if a couple decided to separate there would be public homes and schools for the children. Mothers who would rather do something else than care for their children could put them in the schools, where they would be cared for by women who preferred taking care of children to any other work. In this way we would never have diseased or disabled children from careless and incompetent mothers.

"Besides this," she went on, "in our free schools every child would have a chance to learn and pursue that for which it has ability. Can you imagine the number of children today, children of poor parents, who are born with ability for music or painting, or letters, whose abilities lie dormant for the lack of means and the necessity to work for their daily bread as soon as they are out of their cradles."

Her Relatives.

"Have you any brothers or sisters, Miss Goldman?"

"Yes; a married brother, who does not bother about anything, and only reads the papers when there is something in them about me. My sister is also married and, while not actively engaged in our cause, is bringing up her children to our principles. My father and mother are also living, near Rochester, and, while not Anarchists, sympathize with me and do not interfere with my work."

"What is your future?"

"I cannot say. I shall live to agitate to promote our ideas. I am willing to give my liberty and my life, if necessary, to further my case. It is my mission and I shall not falter."

"Do you think that murder is going to help your cause?"

She looked grave; she shook her head slowly.

"That is a long subject to discuss. I don't believe that through murder we shall gain, but by war, labor against capital, masses against classes, which will not come in twenty or twenty-five years. But some day, I firmly believe, we shall gain, and until then I am satisfied to agitate to teach, and I only ask justice and freedom of speech."

And so I left the little Anarchist, the modern Joan of Arc, waiting patiently in the Tombs until her friends could secure bail for her.

"I shall certainly get a year or a year and a half," she said to me in parting, "not because my offense deserves it, but because I am an Anarchist." [...]

BIOGRAPHICAL TIMELINE

1869	Emma Goldman is born the first of four children to a widow with two daughters, Taube Bienowitch, and her second husband, Abraham Goldman, in Kovno in the Russian Empire (today Kaunas, Lithuania). Abraham Goldman loses Bienowitch's inheritance in a poor business investment and subsequently opens one unsuccessful store after another.
	She suffers poverty, injustice, and oppression at a young age. Her family lives in Jewish ghettoes, migrating frequently to escape anti-Semitism. She witnesses violence against women and children, landlord brutality, and corrupt officials extorting fees from a powerless constituency.
1881	The Goldman family moves to St. Petersburg months after the assassination of Czar Alexander II. Though the Goldman children are forced to work to support the family, Emma pursues an independent education over the strenuous objections of her father who insists on a domestic future for her. As a teenager, she embraces nihilist philosophy.
1885	On December 29, Goldman and her sister Helena arrive in New York City and settle in Rochester where they join their sister Lena and her husband. She works as a seamstress in a clothing factory for a short time. Refused a raise, she quits and takes a job at a smaller shop nearby. She meets and marries Jacob Kershner, a fellow worker. They divorce within a year, briefly reunite when Kershner threatens suicide, but soon separate again.
	Years later she reflects: "I was married […] when I was scarcely seventeen. I suffered—let me say no more about that. I believe in the marriage of affection. That is the only true marriage […] Tell me […] how can a woman go before a minister and take an oath to love 'this man' all her life? How can she tell but to-morrow, next week, she may get to know this man and hate him. Love is founded on respect, and a woman cannot tell what a man is until she lives with him. Instead of being free to end the relationship when her feelings change, she lives on in a state that is the most depraved of all."
1886	Fleeing anti-Semitism, Goldman's parents and brothers join the rest of the family in Rochester.

Goldman is shocked and profoundly influenced by the trial, conviction, and execution of labor activists falsely accused of a bombing in Chicago's Haymarket Square. Their deaths reinforce her attraction to the anti-authoritarian political philosophy of anarchism.

1889   Ostracized by her parents and the Rochester Jewish community, Goldman leaves Rochester for New York City.

On her first day in New York City, she meets Alexander Berkman, who would become her lover and lifelong friend, at Sach's Café, a gathering place for radicals. He invites her to hear Johann Most, the editor of a radical publication called *Freiheit*. Most becomes a mentor and helps cultivate Emma's oratory skills.

1893–4   During the Panic of 1893, Goldman delivers a polemic speech at a protest of nearly three thousand workers in Union Square, in New York City, calling on the unemployed to "demonstrate before the palaces of the rich, demand work. If they do not give you work, demand bread. If they deny you both, take bread."

She is put on trial for incitement to riot and ultimately sentenced to a year's imprisonment in Blackwell's Island Penitentiary. While awaiting trial, she is interviewed by *New York World* journalist Nellie Bly.

In her sympathetic article, Bly calls Goldman "a modern Joan of Arc."

1901–7   On September 6, Leon Czolgosz, an unemployed factory worker and registered Republican with a history of mental illness, shoots President William McKinley, who dies eight days later. During his interrogation he claims that he was inspired to do so after hearing one of Goldman's lectures. Though the police clear Goldman of any connection to Czolgosz, she refuses to condemn him, remarking: "As an anarchist, I am opposed to violence. But if the people want to do away with assassins, they must do away with the conditions which produce murderers."

1903–13   Goldman works as a private nurse under the assumed name of E. G. Smith.

The U.S. Congress passes the Anarchist Exclusion Act of 1903 and arrests the English anarchist John Turner. Goldman joins forces with the Free Speech League to champion his cause.

In 1906, Goldman founds *Mother Earth,* an influential anarchist magazine devoted to politics and literature.

On May 18 of that year, Berkman is released from prison and the two reunite.

1907	Berkman takes the helm of *Mother Earth*, while Goldman tours the country to raise funds to keep it operating.
1917	On June 15, Goldman and Berkman are imprisoned for opposing the World War I draft. Goldman serves two years at the Missouri State Penitentiary in Jefferson City; Berkman spends his prison sentence in Atlanta, Georgia.

In a speech to the jury at her anti-conscription trial, Goldman defends her anarchist principles to the American jury:

"Your Government is allied with the French Republic. Need I call your attention to the historic fact that the great upheaval in France was brought about by extra-legal means? The Dant[on]s, the Robespierres, the Marats, the Herberts [...] were never within the law. But for those great pioneers and rebels, France would have continued under the yoke of the idle Louis XVI, to whom the sport of shooting jack rabbits was more important than the destiny of the people of France."

1919	Upon their release from prison under the 1918 Anarchist Exclusion Act, Goldman and Berkman, along with two hundred and forty-seven others, are deported to Soviet Russia, just as the Bolshevik revolution there begins splintering.
1921–3	In December, profoundly discouraged that the revolution had devolved into despotism and dictatorship, Goldman and Berkman move to Berlin. Goldman writes a series of articles for the *New York World* exposing the harsh political and economic conditions in Russia.
1923	*My Disillusionment with Russia.*
1924	*My Further Disillusionment with Russia.*
	Goldman moves to London.
1925	As the threat of deportation looms, James Colton, a Scottish anarchist Goldman had first met in Glasgow during a speaking tour thirty years prior, offers to marry Goldman to provide her with British citizenship. The couple marry on June 27. The two exchanged correspondences until Colton's death in 1936.
1927	Goldman travels to Canada.
	On August 23, Italian anarchists Nicola Sacco and Bartolomeo Vanzetti are wrongfully convicted and executed for the murder of a guard.
1928–30	With the help of American supporters including H. L. Mencken, Edna St. Vincent Millay, and Peggy Guggenheim, Goldman relocates to France

and writes her autobiography.

1931   *Living My Life, Vol. 1* is published in New York by Alfred A. Knopf to rave critical reviews.

1933   Goldman receives permission to lecture in the United States to speak about drama and her autobiography but not current political events.

1934   *Living My Life, Vol. 2.*

She arrives in New York on February 2, 1934, and is warmly received by friends and much in demand as a lecturer. In May, her U.S. visa expires and Goldman moves to Canada.

1936   On June 28, after six years of extremely ill health and complete dependence on others, Berkman commits suicide at his home in Nice, France.

Goldman turns her attention to the Spanish Civil War. Goldman makes three visits to Spain during the course of the war, acting as publicist and fund-raiser for Spanish anarcho-syndicalists.

Goldman believes the Spanish Civil War crucial to the international struggle against fascism. It is, in her view, the only peasant and working-class revolution ever grow out of anarchist ideals. She later remarks that the Spanish Civil War had influenced her more profoundly than her experience in Russia.

Her Spanish anarchist comrades ask Goldman to direct their English propaganda campaign, designating her the London representative of the National Confederation of Labor and the Iberian Anarchist Federation (CNT-FAI). She works tirelessly, writing hundreds of letters to supporters and editors in the English-speaking world.

1939   Goldman devotes the last year of her life to securing political asylum and financial support for the women and children refugees of the Spanish war and to publicizing legislative dangers to free speech in Canada.

1940   On May 14, Emma Goldman dies of a stroke in Toronto, Canada. The U.S. Immigration and Naturalization Service allows her body to be brought back to the United States. She is buried in German Waldheim Cemetery (now named Forest Home Cemetery) in Forest Park, Illinois, near the graves of those executed after the Haymarket affair.

Made in United States
Cleveland, OH
13 February 2025

14327111R00080